The MORBID CURIOUS

The
MORBID
CURIOUS
No. 1

Esteemed Mortals...

Welcome to the very first edition of The Morbid Curious, a journal from American Hauntings Ink that is committed to bringing you tales of ghosts, hauntings, true crime, and the unexplained from the haunted history of America. This first edition is a bit of an experiment, but we hope that you'll enjoy what we have to offer within these pages and will consider submitting something of your own for one of the books to come.

The idea of the "Morbid Curious" came during the recording of the Villisca Ax Murder season of the American Hauntings Podcast. In reference to one of the murders committed by the roving Billy the Axman, a newspaper reporter in Colorado made a note of the crowds of "the morbid curious" that came to view one of the crime scenes. There was something that struck me about the name, and I pledged that I would find a way to use it - and two years later, I did.

Hopefully, you'll find that it was worth the wait.

We'll be back in the spring with our Walpurgisnacht edition, but if you have any questions, comments, or want to send in material, you can reach us at the email address on page six.

Thanks again for being part of our first edition - we plan to have many more to come!

Troy Taylor
Harvest 2020

IN THIS EDITION

Editor and Art Director
Troy Taylor

Cover Art Designer
April Slaughter

Contact
ghosts@americanhauntings.net

This Book is Published By:
American Hauntings Ink
Jacksonville, Illinois | 217.791.7859
Visit us on the Internet at http://www.americanhauntingsink.com

First Edition - October 2020

Printed in the United States of America

THE HAUNTED RESTAURANT TRIFECTA IN THE WITCH CITY

Amanda R. Woomer * Spook Eats

Few places in America have a dark mark on its history quite like the small coastal town of Salem, Massachusetts. For several months in 1692, a gaggle of girls brought Salem to the edge of mass hysteria, leading to 200 accusations and 20 wrongful executions.

Today, the Witch City has gone beyond embracing their past—they have found ways of honoring the victims of America's worst -- but not only -- witch hunt without glorifying the horrors. But Salem has also gone one step further than that. The city has created a welcoming environment for people from all walks of life, including those of different sexual orientations and religions. Many believe that the atmosphere is so welcoming that some visitors refuse to leave... even after death.

Alongside New Orleans and Savannah, Salem is considered one of America's weirdest cities, home to haunted history and haunted places. Luckily for us, some of those haunted locations aren't abandoned, dreary, or condemned—they're restaurants, ready

to share in their spirits of all kinds with anyone brave enough to visit.

Turner's Seafood

The history of Turner's Seafood goes well beyond the brick façade you see today on Church Street. You see, the land that you're enjoying that lobster roll on was once the apple orchard of Bridget Bishop.

Bridget is most famously

remembered for being the first person executed as a witch in Salem, but her reputation went beyond poppets and the Devil's Mark. She was an outsider, a brash woman who liked to swear, drink, and play games -- she actually sounds awesome, if you ask me. According to court records, Bridget Bishop *"did entertaine people in her house at unseasonable houres in the night to keep drinking and playing at shovel-board."* This and the word of a few children and unhappy neighbors was enough to seal her fate. Bridget was hanged as a witch, and, today, her apple orchard is no more. But many say the land's original owner is certainly not resting peacefully.

Since 1989, patrons and staff have reported seeing a woman wandering around the building now home to Turner's Seafood in a flowing white dress. Some refer to her as their Lady in White, but most feel the apparition is that of Bridget Bishop, returning to her beloved orchard. Accompanying Bridget is the overwhelming smell of apples in the restaurant, on the sidewalk, and even in the breezeway behind the building, leading to Essex Street... all where her apple orchard once stood. Despite Bridget's tragic and grisly end, she is not a vengeful spirit. In fact, she likes to play games with visitors, stealing spoons to the point where the wait staff will have to bring you a new spoon four or five times! My question is: where do all those spoons go?

Speaking of spoons, you'll need them to enjoy their lobster bisque. It's easily the best thing on their menu, as well as their signature cocktail Bridget's Orchard. It's a twist on a big kid's apple cider created in honor of their signature ghost. Cheers to that!

Rockafella's

The always hoppin' Rockafella's might not have direct ties to the Salem Witch Trials. After all, the building itself was only built in 1826. However, many people blame the haunting on the land that it sits on.

Many visitors and residents of Salem believe Essex Street is one of the most haunted roads in the United States. According to stories, the condemned would be carted down Essex Street to Gallow's Hill on the western side of town, but not before stopping at the church -- where Rockafella's now stands -- to be excommunicated.

Like so many places in Salem, Rockafella's claims to be haunted... but not by anyone associated with the witch trials.

Their most famous entity is the Lady in Blue. What a breath of fresh air! Finally, someone dressing in something other than white! No one knows who this mystery lady is, but she is seen so often that the restaurant has created a cocktail in her honor. And yes, it is blue.

But the Lady in Blue isn't the only spirit wandering through the historic building turned popular restaurant. There is a much darker entity that lurks on the upper floors.

He's described as an older man dressed all in black and tends to lash out towards women, sometimes even

pushing them violently. It's believed he was a former minister when the building was used as a church.

While you're enjoying your flatbread pizzas or Bloody Mary -- complete with meat straw! -- don't be too concerned if you hear footsteps, banging, or talking coming from the basement. There's a series of tunnels supposedly connected to the days of the Underground Railroad that run underneath the entire city, and ghostly activity runs rampant down there...

Mercy Tavern

Speaking of underground tunnels!

Mercy Tavern is a bit off the beaten path in Salem, situated on Derby Street, also on top of a series of tunnels. And while Essex Street is far more famous with its occult shops, psychic mediums, and museums, Derby Street has its own dark and dirty history.

After the trauma of the witch trials, Salem developed its red-light district, and Derby Street was at the

heart of it. According to stories, captains of various ships would shanghai young men enjoying themselves at the bars and brothels of Derby Street, including the building that is now Mercy Tavern. The stories go even further, telling of pirates that would use the underground tunnels to move discreetly from the waterfront through the city.

Today, there isn't much left of Salem's seedier days. Mercy Tavern is a proud farm to table tavern with a rotating menu of meals and cocktails.

To make your visit even more appetizing, they truly are living up to their name. A portion of each bill is donated to a local charity or organization in the Salem community.

But even though Mercy Tavern has tried to revitalize the building's reputation, those tunnels are still filled with deep dark secrets and maybe even a few ghosts.

Much of Derby Street and Derby Wharf is considered to be haunted, but Mercy Tavern seems to be the epicenter.

Staff and diners have reported the ghostly apparitions of pirates appearing in the bar area, no doubt searching for their delicious Wharf Punch! There are also tales of the sound of shouting and fighting coming from the tunnels below.

My advice? Order one of their signature cocktails. Make sure it's got rum in it. And make sure to pour out a sip for one of the pirates lurking in Mercy Tavern.

Whether you're searching for rich history, delicious food and drink, or a haunting atmosphere, Salem has it all. Ghosts don't just haunt this small ocean-side town—history does too—and should remind us that sometimes, it's the living we need to fear, rather than the dead.

THE CONTROVERSIAL CORPSE OF BUFFALO BILL

Troy Taylor

There is no question that William "Buffalo Bill" Cody is one of the icons of the American West. Born near LeClaire, Iowa, in 1846, Cody began riding to the Pony Express when he was 14. He fought in the Civil War, served as a scout for the Army, and was already a legend when he started his famous Wild West show, which traveled the United States and Europe. He was a larger-than-life character who turned the American frontier experienced into popular entertainment - but the story of Bill's body and its many burials that is even more outrageous than the man himself.

Cody was just a 13-year-old boy in Iowa, working for a freight company as a messenger when he decided that he wanted to be a prospector in the Pikes Peak gold rush of 1859. The next year, he joined the Pony Express. He fit the bill for the advertised positions - he was a "skinny, expert rider willing to risk death daily."

He later served during the Civil War and, in 1867, began buffalo hunting to feed the work crews that were building the railroads. This job gave him the nickname that he'd have for the remainder of his life. By his own estimate, he killed more than 4,200 buffalo over the next year and a half.

Cody returned to work for the Army as chief of scouts in 1868, earning him the Congressional Medal of Honor four years later, all the while becoming a national folk hero, thanks to the dime-novel exploits of "Buffalo Bill," written by Ned Buntline. In late 1872, he went to Chicago and made his debut in Buntline's Wild West show, "The Scouts of the Prairie." The next year, "Wild Bill Hickok" joined the show for a time, and the entire troupe toured for the next 10 years.

In 1883, Cody founded his own show, "Buffalo Bill's Wild West," a circus-like extravaganza that featured horses, trick shooting, "wild" Indians, and faux stagecoach robberies. It toured widely for three decades in the United States and later in Europe. Besides Buffalo Bill himself, the show starred sharpshooter Annie Oakley and, for one run, Chief Sitting Bull.

Sadly, in January 1917, Bill died from kidney failure. His corpse ended up on a mountain outside of Denver, Colorado, which seemed odd considering his close ties to the town in Wyoming that had been named for him - Cody. It had been founded in the 1890s with help from Bill, who'd employed many of its residents and was responsible for most of its tourist business. It might seem natural for him to be buried in a place that he knew and loved so much, but he wasn't.

And that's where the trouble began.

Bill had loved the town of Cody, but he also loved Colorado. His first adventure had been looking for gold at Pike's Peak, and his traveling show had brought him back to Colorado often. His sister lived in Denver, so he frequently visted her there. He died there, too, and before he did, he told his wife that he wanted to be buried in Golden, Colorado, on Lookout Mountain.

But weather almost derailed Bill's burial plans. He died in January, which meant the road to Lookout Mountain was impassable, and the spot where he wanted to be laid to rest was frozen solid. First, though, his body was displayed at the Colorado Capitol building, where he was eulogized by the governor and his many famous friends. This his body traveled in a carriage through the streets of Denver, where thousands lined up to say goodbye. Finally, his remains were placed in cold storage until the weather changed.

Meanwhile, a heated feud had erupted between Colorado and Wyoming over the body of one of the most famous men in America. Wyoming - citing an early draft of Cody's will - said that he intended to be buried there. Colorado cried foul, however, because Cody's final will left his burial location up to his widow, who chose Lookout Mountain, following her dying husband's wishes. Rumors began to circulate that a group of men from Wyoming had stolen Bill's body from the mortuary and swapped it with the body of a local vagrant.

Hoping to stop the rumors, Bill was finally buried in an open casket on Lookout Mountain in June 1917. More than 25,000 people journeyed to the mountain to bid him farewell. To prevent the theft of his body, Bill's bronze casket was sealed in a tamper-proof vault, then it was encased in concrete and iron.

But, of course, that's not the end of the story.

There were some people who would do anything to get Bill's body back to Wyoming, including his niece, Mary Jester Allen. In the 1920s, she began making public claims that the state of Colorado had tampered with her uncle's will, falsifying his wishes about his burial place. In response, Cody's foster son, Johnny Baker, had the body exhumed and then reburied at the same site under several tons of concrete. Baker already owned a museum dedicated to Buffalo Bill in Colorado. Allen soon opened a competing one in Wyoming.

Things got even stranger after that. In 1948, the American Legion in Cody, Wyoming, offered a $10,000 reward to anyone who would disinter the body and bring it to Wyoming. This

The burial site On Cedar Mountain in Wyoming where some conspiracists say Buffalo Bill is actually buried.

led to Colorado National Guard troops being assigned to keep watch over the grave.

Since then, things have remained calm between the two states, despite the humorous debate in the Wyoming legislature about stealing the body in 2006. In 2020, Buffalo Bill remains safe and sound in his Colorado grave.

That's the official story, anyway.

Some folks in Wyoming claim otherwise. They say that Bill was never buried on Lookout Mountain at all, so there was no need to steal him. The body was smuggled out of Denver after his death and buried up on Cedar Mountain, outside Cody, where he originally wanted to be interred.

Truth or fiction? We'll likely never know.

A VISITOR 'ROUND MIDNIGHT

Trevelyn Florence-Thomas

The morning of July 6, 2017 started off like any other. It was a sunny Thursday, and it was time for me to make my commute to work. I arrived at the office a little before 8:30am and reported to my cubicle to get my day started. I had a phone conference scheduled for around 10:00am, and I needed to prepare. That's when my cell phone rang, and I answered it. I'll never forget the sound of despair and anguish in my youngest brother's voice, "Sis!! Sis!! Mom won't wake up!" My brother was wailing. I immediately responded, "Bro, call 911!" He answered, "I did...she's cold. Sis...she's gone." As my brother continued to sob, I told him, "I'll be there as soon as I can." At that point, my entire existence shifted into autopilot, as symptoms of disassociation began to creep in. I notified my supervisor that I had a family emergency and swiftly made my way to my vehicle. It was a bright and beautiful day for a forty-minute commute. However, during the entire drive, I remember thinking...she's gone...she's really gone...forever. I will always remember that day as if it were yesterday. Of the things I most recollect, she looked at peace and as if she were merely sleeping. The next thing I recall most is the stiffness and coldness of her cheek against my lips when I bent over and kissed her for the last time.

My mother had been diagnosed with Multiple Sclerosis in 2009. I relocated back to my hometown of Jacksonville, IL, from Nashville, TN, not long before she had received the devastating news. As her oldest child and only daughter, I became her caregiver. Hence, that responsibility had been a priority in my life for the past eight years, prior to her death. I literally loved my mother 'til death. We had been very close and endured some very difficult times together. My mother died of a massive heart attack at home, in the house she loved so much. Her soul departed from this earth a week from her upcoming birthday on July 15th.

My youngest brother, his fiancé, and their children now live in our family home. Nonetheless, I can still feel my mother's presence when I cross the threshold and enter the front door of that house. Even now, it gives me goosebumps to think of it. She would never speak much on the topic during her life, but I knew; my mom had spiritual gifts and an uncanny ability to discern things about people, places, and situations. The reason I know is that she and I shared the same gift, along with my maternal grandmother.

Several weeks had passed since her death. It was close to midnight. I had settled into bed for the evening and drifted into the light sleep stage. Suddenly, I felt a presence enter my room. My heartbeat increased. Next came the goosebumps. Then, I felt a subtle, sinking sensation in the middle part of the bottom of my mattress. My eyes immediately popped open, and I inhaled deeply. Whatever it was that just entered my room had sat down on my bed. Positioned on my left side, I exhaled the breath I had been holding, reluctantly raised my head off the pillow, and slowly turned to look over my right shoulder. That's when I saw something, or rather, someone. In the darkness, my eyes descried a silhouette sitting at the foot of my bed. The head

Geneva Elizabeth Florence Harris

July 15, 1953–July 6, 2017

slowly turned to the left, as if to peer back at me over the left shoulder. The curve of her cheek...the same one I had kissed, the length of her neck, the coif of her hair, the fullness of her shoulders, the roundness of her back; it was her! It was my mom.

Stunned and shaken, yet not overly afraid, I whispered, "I felt that. I felt you sit down. What are you doing here?!" At that point, I sensed the weight lift from my bed. In the darkness, I could see tiny glints of light as I squinted intensively. I detected the energy as it exited my bedroom, and with a gentle rush of air, her manifestation was gone. That was my first encounter with my mother's spirit, and I am quite confident that it will not be my last.

Until then, may her soul be at peace.

THE "SHOE CITY" FACTORY DISASTER

Rene Kruse

Brockton, Massachusetts: 1905

For nearly a century, Brockton, Massachusetts, was known as "Shoe City." In the early 1830s, shoe manufacturers found a home in Brockton, known then as Bridgewater, though no one knew exactly why. By the end of the 1830s there had been over 200 shoe patents filed with the US Patent Office that had been developed in Bridgewater/Brockton. During the Civil War, Brockton was the largest producer of shoes in America and the world's leading shoe center. Brockton furnished the footwear for the Union army, as well as nearly everyone in the northern states. By 1907, the largest number of highly skilled shoemakers in the world lived in Brockton, and over 20,000 people were employed by 39 different shoe manufacturers. The decline of Brockton's shoe industry began during the Great Depression when hundreds of thousands of people could no longer afford to buy new shoes, and many shoe companies left town in search of cheaper labor. In 1969, only 10 companies remained in Brockton and employed just 2,000 people. A tremendous decline for what was once the world's "Shoe City."

Brockton has experienced a great rise and equally great fall in the world of shoes, but in 1905, the shoe industry was at its peak. The two largest shoe manufacturers in town were the W.L. Douglas Co. and the George E. Keith Co., known as the "Bookends of Brockton." By comparison, the R. B. Grover Shoe Co. may not have been the largest, but it was certainly close. Grover wanted to produce fashionable and comfortable shoes that were affordable to the general public. In his push for quality in design and materials, he created the Emerson Shoes brand. For many years, Emerson Shoes were considered to be the best shoes made in the country and were becoming more popular by the day. Grover had 33 stores already in place but plans to open dozens more were in the works.

Robins Grover operated his Grover Shoe Factory in a large industrial building on the corner of Main and Calmar Streets in the Campello section of Brockton. The factory, which took up half a city block, was in the shape of a capital E. The giant boiler keeping the huge building warm was located in the boiler pit (also known as the boiler house) at the end of the center bar of the E. Originally, the building had three floors, but Emerson shoes had become so popular that Grover had added a fourth floor to keep up with the demand. The largest and heaviest pieces of equipment were located on the top three floors.

Grover was a unique employer for his time. He wanted to make money, just like his fellow manufacturers, but he was also concerned for his employees. He paid them a reasonable wage and made sure that their workspaces were clean and well ventilated. As a result, his people were loyal and dedicated. With his top of the line shoe manufacturing equipment and more than 400 hard-working employees, his factory was shipping out 56,000 cases of shoes each month. When Grover opened the books

Typical early twentieth-century shoe factory worker

for March 1905, he was planning to increase production even further.

When the factory building had been expanded by adding a fourth floor, the old coal-fired boiler, which had provided the steam that fed the radiators throughout the factory, was no longer sufficient for the job. A new, larger boiler was installed, but the old boiler was left in place in case they needed a backup. Chief engineer David Rockwell was in charge of the operation and maintenance of both boilers. He had several other duties in

The R.B. Grover Shoe Factory in the early 1900s

early that morning so that he could get the building comfortably warm by the time the workers arrived for their day-shift. At 7:45 AM, less than an hour into the shift, the plant manager called Rockwell with concerns about some strange noises that were coming from the radiators along the one wall. Rockwell had stepped out, but his assistant tried to put the manager's mind at ease and told him that everything was fine.

Three minutes later, the boiler blew with the explosive force equivalent to 660 pounds of dynamite. The boiler itself was shot from the boiler pit like a rocket, bursting through the four floors above, killing anyone in its path. It was propelled in an almost straight line into the air, before arcing to the north, at which time it slammed into a water tower over that part of the building. The heavy tower fell, slamming down onto the roof, causing a large portion of the building to collapse. One floor pancaked onto the next floor until much of the building had been flattened with the walls

the factory, but he believed that watching over the boilers was his most demanding and the most important responsibility.

The new boiler was totally adequate and worked well, so the old boiler was rarely used, but when it was, Rockwell was always uneasy. He would have preferred to have it removed and be done with it. But there were occasions when he agreed that there was a need. The new boiler did need to be flushed occasionally as part of its routine maintenance.

The Monday morning of March 20, 1905 was a cold and damp one. Rockwell was going to be performing maintenance on the new boiler, so he fired up the old one and put it back in service for the day. He had come in falling inward. Between 300 and 400 employees were in the factory at the time of the explosion.

Many workers survived the collapse of the building when wall and ceiling sections were kept from crushing them by heavy broken beams and wrecked equipment. The same beams and machines that had saved many of them from the collapse would prove to cause their deaths as the disaster progressed. Several dozen people were trapped inside the wreckage when they became pinned down by the very devices that had saved them.

When the boiler had exploded out from the boiler pit, it brought with it a shower of hot, burning coals that were scattered across the debris from the collapse. The coals started a hundred small fires, but they had not become a severe hazard - yet.

Over 100 of the employees had escaped from the collapsed building uninjured. Most of them ran right back in to help free their coworkers who had become trapped or tangled in by the wreckage. The employee rescuers were soon joined by people from the neighborhood. The firefighters from the Campello district fire department were on the scene within minutes as their firehouse was directly behind the Grover factory building. The many rescuers moved rapidly through the ruins, searching for victims and freeing them when they could. The possibility of a rapidly spreading fire loomed large in their minds.

Several men and women who found themselves trapped in the section of the building that remained standing became panic-stricken. The initial explosion had been so fierce that the fire escapes had been blown away from the building. These people didn't know if their section might collapse at any second, crushing them under the rubble, or if the fire would reach up and snatch up their lives before they could be rescued. Many of them, in a desperate attempt to save their own lives, or possibly to end their lives quickly and painlessly, jumped from the second, third, and fourth story windows. Most of these people did survive the fall, but if any of them were hoping for a painless way out, they were sadly mistaken. All of those who had jumped were severely injured.

The ruins of the building were primed for a fire. The collapse had broken or cracked many of the gas lines creating dozens of leaks. The wooden floors were treated with linseed oil every night to keep the dust down, leaving the floors in a highly flammable state. The blast had blown out over 300 windows, and much of the roof had collapsed, so the fire would be well ventilated. All of these factors added up to a massive conflagration that would soon eat through the debris of the wood frame building. But there was to be one more horrible surprise that morning.

The R.B. Grover Shoe Factory after the fire. The only part left standing was the smokestack.

A wooden shed behind the boiler house was used to store several barrels of the chemical naphtha, a volatile industrial solvent. When the hot coals showered down over the debris, a few fell onto the shed, which quickly caught fire. As the shed burned around the barrels, they heated until they too exploded. Sheets of flaming naphtha showered down upon and around the rescuers, driving them back as the heat rapidly became unbearable.

The roof had been blown off or collapsed across the entire building creating a "chimney effect," and the fires, which were small and scattered, had combined to form a raging beast, rendering everything in its path to charred wreckage and ashes. An abundance of flammable materials and chemicals, coupled with the free flow of oxygen, caused the fire to burn faster and hotter than any the local fire department had ever experienced. The workers who had somehow survived the first explosion and collapse suddenly found themselves held prisoner "beneath heavy timbers, flooring, and thousands of pounds of the latest shoe manufacturing equipment." They were left helpless and hopeless as they watched the hungry flames eat their way toward them.

Undaunted by the flames, many rescuers ran back into the ruin to save as many of the trapped victims as they could. Working in small teams, they used long beams and timbers as levers to pry the wreckage from the bodies of the living, so they might escape. Some were able to run out, but others had to be carried. Many of these daring men ran back into the wreckage several times, not willing to leave anyone behind to face the fiery death that awaited them. One such hero was Firefighter Moore, who ran inside with nothing but an ax, which he used to chop away at timbers as the fire loomed close enough to singe his hair.

He saved three people before he was finally forced back by the heat.

Another hero that day was Rev. James A. O'Rourke, the priest from St. Margaret's Roman Catholic Church, located across the street from the Grover Shoe Factory. Father O'Rourke was one of the first in the neighborhood to arrive after the explosion. He had run into the ruins several times and had saved seven of the trapped workers. By that time, the fire was out of control, and the smoke was black and dense. As Father O'Rourke ran toward the building an eighth time, he fainted from exhaustion and smoke inhalation. When he awoke a few minutes later, he found that there was nothing else he could do, so he moved among the injured, administering the Catholic last rites to anyone who appeared near death. Father O'Rourke gave an account of his experience to a *New York Times* reporter the following day:

"Pinned beneath heavy pieces of machinery, timbers, and twisted coils of pipe were many poor men and women suffering terrible agonies. In order to reach these imprisoned sufferers we had to crawl through the debris. With the aid of a large timber we raised the wreckage which held fast several men and women, and in this manner and by brute strength, pulled out seven employees.

By this time the flames were almost upon us, and we were about to flee for safety, when one poor fellow begged that a last effort be made to save him. Three of us grasped the man by the shoulders and arms and tugged and pulled until suddenly he cried: 'My God, my leg is pulled off'. It was especially terrible because a moment later, with our clothing scorched, we were ordered away by the Chief of the Fire Department, and were compelled to leave the poor man to his fate.

Just before leaving I saw at least fifteen of the poor imprisoned people, some already suffering untold agonies from the flames and others watching them with terror-stricken eyes, knowing that a moment or two would bring to them similar suffering, and then death."

There were as many acts of self-sacrifice as there were of heroism. An unknown woman who was tangled in a mass of machinery was found by a team of rescuers. She begged them to leave her and find others that could be saved. Crying, she told them that she was already dying, and there was no hope for her, but maybe for someone else... As the men moved on, she begged to be shot, but that was not within their

Four acres of death and destruction

ability, and she was soon consumed by the fire.

Mr. George Smith awoke after being stunned into unconsciousness by the explosion, only to find he was hopelessly pinned between heavy pieces of equipment. A rescue team arrived to try to free him, but he believed there was no way they could lift the machine resting across his legs and feet. Instead, using only his arms, he lifted several people (including his own nephew) over the machines and into the arms of waiting firemen. Mr. Smith remained behind, awaiting his fiery doom, as those victims he had just saved ran to safety.

Dozens of similar stories came out of the disaster. Rescuers told of people who were too deep in the ruins or under too much debris to be freed in time to be saved. Knowing they would not survive, they shouted encouragement to men as they worked to free the people they could reach. Then, they spoke calming words to friends and coworkers around them as they waited to die. These brave people met their inevitable fate with a brave face. Their bodies were found later, roasted from the searing heat of the flames.

As the fire had been transformed from a threatening aggravation to a giant inferno, strong winds carried the flames and burning debris across Calmar Street, here it consumed a three-story building housing a hardware store, a boarding house, a home, and three small businesses. Not yet satisfied, the cinders and flames were carried by the wind across Denton Street, where they destroyed three more family homes. The fire left in its wake four acres of death and utter destruction.

Over 200 workers had found their way outside, either unharmed or with mild injuries. Some of them didn't know what to do, so they wandered home. The mayor of Brockton sent requests out all over town, asking that anyone who had survived the explosion and fire would please report to the police station and give their names. The police later told of one young man who was in such a state of shock that when he stumbled from the wreckage, he went to another shoe factory, applied for a job, and worked there the rest of the day. When he returned home that evening, he found that his family was in mourning for him, believing him to be among the dead.

The fire raged through the ruins and surrounding buildings with such great speed and energy that people were able to enter parts of the ruins later that afternoon. The firemen, policemen, and volunteers moved through the rubble, searching for bodies. They were often so overcome after viewing the wretched conditions of the people they once knew, that they had to leave the wreckage to regain their composure. In the area of the boiler house, they found badly burned and headless bodies. It was supposed that these people had been in the path of the boiler as it blasted through the building. There they also found random human bones scattered about the area of the boiler house, victims of a direct hit by the explosive blast.

As the search continued, a mystery began to surface. No one had been able to find David Rockwell, the chief engineer and the man who had been responsible for the operation of the boilers. Rumors spread faster than the fire had. Some thought that he was injured and had been taken to the hospital in bandages, unrecognized. Others agreed that he would be found among the dead as the ruins were searched. But one story seemed to be gaining a following; that he had been away from the building when the boiler had exploded, and when he saw what had happened, he had left town either

The boiler finally came to rest in the home of Mrs. Etta Hood, located just north of the factory

in shame or to escape accusations of blame. His wife was found and asked if she could shed light on the mystery. She told the police that just before the explosion, she had looked out her kitchen window and had seen her husband sitting in a chair just outside the boiler house door. Several men were sent to search that area, and they found the crushed, charred body of a man who they believed to be Rockwell.

In an ironic twist, after the rocketing boiler had toppled the water tower, it continued on its destructive path, which took it in an arc, up and over the north half of the building. As the boiler returned to the ground, it smashed through a house, leaving it demolishing, then pierced a second house, where it finally came to rest. The house that was destroyed by the crashing boiler was that of Mr. and Mrs. David Rockwell - the very same David Rockwell who had fired up the boiler that very morning. Mrs. Rockwell had been bending over the

The 39 unidentified victims were laid to rest in a mass grave in Melrose Cemetery in Brockton.

stove in her kitchen when the boiler passed by her, missing her by only a few feet. She miraculously survived, as did her two children. She found them in the wreckage of her own home and ran to her neighbor's home, that of Mrs. Etta Hood. To her surprise, she found that the boiler had come to rest, half in and half out of Mrs. Hood's home. It almost seemed as if after killing Mr. Rockwell, the boiler had gone off in search of Mrs. Rockwell.

The entire city of Brockton was in mourning. In all, 58 of her citizens had been brutally and violently killed. A few of the dead were not employees of the shoe factory but instead had been killed while inside one of the seven other buildings taken by the fire. Over 150 people were moderate to severely injured, and the hospitals were full. The fire took its last victim on April 15th, when Hiram Pierce lost his battle for life.

Because of the fire's extreme heat, only a few of the bodies could be positively identified. Some were identified only by the position of their bodies linked with the memories of rescuers who had seen them trapped there. Most of the bodies were never identified. Their remains were carefully placed in coffins as they were removed from the ruins of the factory and taken to a building in downtown Brockton.

The Brockton City Council purchased a large lot in Brockton's Melrose Cemetery and had a granite memorial stone prepared with the names of those who had died. The remains of 39 unidentified people were buried in a mass grave. Their coffins were placed in a circle, with each radiating out from the center like the spokes in a wheel. The monument was placed in the center.

The day after the fire, the leatherworkers union announced that the injured factory employees would receive $5 a week until they were recovered enough to return to work. Death benefits of $100 were paid to the families of everyone who was killed.

The mayor set up the Brockton Relief Fund to provide support for the victims of the fire. Money poured in from around the country. A total of $105,000 in cash was collected and distributed according to need.

An investigation into the cause of the disaster resulted in a somewhat unsatisfactory finding. The final report stated that the blame lay in the improper manufacture of the old boiler and the fault was in such a place as to be undetectable. No blame was placed on Mr. Rockwell or Mr. Grover. Between 1880 and 1890, there had been over 2,000 boiler explosions, and safety had improved somewhat. In 1905, when the Grover Shoe Factory's boiler exploded, there were well over 100,000 boilers in operation around the country. The dramatic loss of life in Brockton brought public attention to the problem, and work began to pass laws to enforce safer designs and operations.

Mr. Robbins Grover did not rebuild the Grover Shoe Factory, and the company was soon in bankruptcy. Mr. Grover never recovered from the great loss of life in his factory. He was not as much affected by the loss of his business as he was by the loss of his employees, each of which he cared about deeply. He spent the rest of his life working toward collecting money to provide additional financial aid to the families of the dead and injured. Mr. Grover died a broken man. He told his friends privately that he was tormented by the people who had died in and around his factory and rarely slept through the night. He worked to atone for their loss in the hope that he would one day find peace.

The city of Brockton was left with a lingering type of presence. The land upon which the Grover Shoe Factory once stood, and the surrounding buildings taken by the fire, was thought to have taken on a shadow of sorts. People naturally avoided the site for many years. The entire area was said to smell of burned timbers and leather for decades, long after the burned materials had been removed. And then, there was that strange smell in the area of the cemetery which contained the mass grave for those killed in the fire. For many, many years after the burials of the victims and the last of the funerals, when the wind blew from a certain direction, passersby might catch a whiff of what they described as the smell of charred, rotting meat, with no discernable source for the odor. It is not a pleasant reminder, but it is a reminder indeed of the tragedy that took place there and the lives that were snuffed out. Those lingering remnants of the fire have faded, and the survivors and witnesses are long gone, but one may believe that the victims lost so long ago had tried hard to keep their memories alive. The phantom odors ceased many years ago, and we hope the dead are finally settled and at peace.

Weird History

"FLU JULIA"
THE FELONIOUS PANDEMIC NURSE

Troy Taylor

In September 1918, a 23-year-old woman named Julia Lyons - also as Marie Walker, Ruth Hicks, Mrs. H. J. Behrens, and a range of other aliases - was arrested at the LaSalle Hotel in Chicago, Illinois, after a crime spree that included posing as a Department of Justice representative, cashing stolen checks, and petty larceny. But the police underestimated their prisoner, and she escaped from the South Clark Street station before charges could be filed.

But her very brief time in jail certainly didn't teach her any lessons. Soon after her escape, he came up with an even more devious method of making money.

In the fall of 1918, Chicago was gripped by the 1918 Spanish Influenza pandemic, and hospitals began recruiting nurses who could tend to patients in their homes. Julia correctly assumed that healthcare officials would not be looking at the credentials of volunteers too closely, so she registered as a nurse under several of her

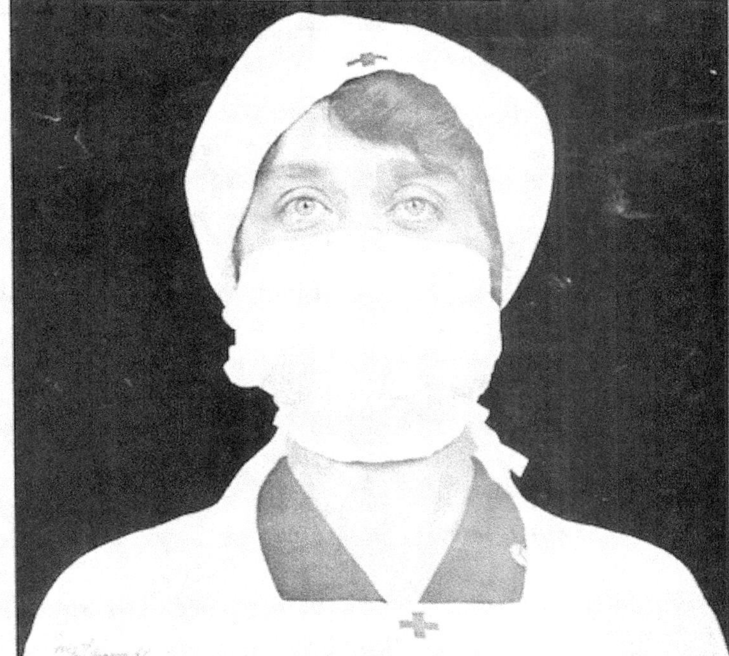

pseudonyms. She was quickly hired and spent the next two months caring for sick men and women all over the city.

Julia's plan was simple. When she filled a prescription for her client, she'd charge them much more than the actual cost. Once, she charged $63 for a dose of oxygen that had cost her $5 - which is the equivalent of charging over $1,000 for a $65 item today. Sometimes, "Flu Julia," as the *Chicago Tribune* would later nickname her, even summoned a doctor to wrote prescriptions for her. That "doctor" was later identified by the police as a "dope seller and narcotic supplier." Once Julia had milked the patient for everything she could get, she fled the home with spare cash, loose jewelry, clothing, and any other valuables she could find.

You might think this was a small price to pay for being nursed back to health after a deadly disease, but Julia didn't do any actual nursing. Once when 9-year-old Eddie Rogan fetched her to help his older brother George, who was "out of his head with illness," Julia retorted, "Oh, let him rave. He's used to raving." George died; Julia could not have cared less.

But Julia wasn't always so pitiless, on the surface, at least. She often fabricated charming stories to win over her patients. She gained the confidence

Cook County Courthouse in the early 1900s

of "old Father Shelhauer" when she asked him, "Don't you remember me? Why when I was a little girl, I used to hitch on your wagons." Shelauer believed her and managed to throw off a detective who was looking for the young woman by vouching for her and saying that he had known her since she was a little girl.

Julia's scheme was never meant to last, though. In November, detectives linked her to Eva Jacobs, another "girl of the shady world," and wiretapped the house of "Suicide Bess" Davis, where Jacobs was living. By listening in, they discovered Julia's plan to marry a restaurant owner named Charlie. They trailed Charlie, who unknowingly led them to his soon-to-be bride.

"The wedding's all bust up! You got me!" Julie cried as the detectives surrounded her. They hauled the couple the police station, where they asked a bewildered Charlie how long he had known Julie. "Ten days!" he said. "That is, I thought I knew her."

When it came time for Julia to appear in court, Deputy Sheriff John Hickey volunteered to transport her there.

Chief Bailiff John Ryan told Hickey, "Be careful, she's pretty slick. Don't let her get away." That warning was also repeated by detectives Robert Jacobs and Frank Smith, who had first arrested Julia at the LaSalle Hotel. They told him about her previous escape from the South Clark station.

Detective Jacobs advised him, "She'll go if she gets a chance. Better put the irons on."

Hickey just chuckled. "Oh, she won't get away from me," he said.

He was wrong.

Hickey did manage to get Julia to the courthouse, where about 50 of her victims testified against her, but about an hour-and-a-half after he was supposed to bring her back to jail, the police received a frantic call from Hickey. Bad news - Julia had jumped out of his moving vehicle and into a getaway car that sped off so quickly that Hickey was unable to chase it down.

But when other detectives started looking a little more closely at Hickey's story, it started to seem fishy. For one thing, he mentioned that they had stopped at a bank so that Julia could withdraw some cash, leading investigators to believe that Hickey might have accepted a bribe to set her free.

Also, the spot where Hickey claimed Julia had jumped from the car was not even close to the route he was supposed to take from the courthouse to the jail. Furthermore, a friend of Julia's named Pearl Auldridge confessed to the police that the plan had been prearranged with Deputy Hickey. He was suspended while detectives went back to searching for Julia.

Finally, in March 1919, after digging through nursing registries, detectives fond Julia - using the name Mrs. James -- at a house on Fullerton Avenue, where she was caring for a woman with influenza. She was easily taken into custody.

In addition to her previous counts of larceny, "obtaining money by false pretenses," and "conducting a confidence game," Julia was also charged with bigamy. She was still married to poor Charlie the restaurant owner, but she had also found another husband, a soldier named E.M. James. She had known him for a whopping four days.

Without a dirty cop to help her escape again, Julia was at the mercy of the criminal justice system. She continued to scheme until the final days of the trial. First she claimed that she had been forced into committing crimes against her will by a "band of thieves" who took advantage of her and then, as a last resort, she tried to please insanity.

She didn't convince anyone. The jury found her guilty of larceny, and the judge sentenced her to serve up to 10 years in the penitentiary. She traded her nurse's uniform for a prison uniform and vanished into the system.

What became of "Flu Julia" after her release is unknown, but it seems unlikely that either of her husbands was waiting for her when she got out.

THE PHANTOM OF HAZEL HILL

Michelle L. Hamilton

In 1793, John Minor built for his new bride a mansion in Fredericksburg, Virginia, that he named Hazel Hill. Hazel Hill was the center of approximately 37 acres of gardens and farmland that stretched from Princess Anne Street to the Rappahannock River. John Minor was born on May 13, 1761, at Topping Castle, in Caroline County, Virginia. At the age of 15, Minor ran away from the College of William & Mary to join the army and fight for his country's independence in the Revolutionary War. Minor served with distinction, and after the war, he returned to William & Mary and studied law under George Wythe.

After the completion of his studies, Minor moved to Fredericksburg and established a successful law practice and became Fredericksburg's first Commonwealth's Attorney. Minor served as a colonel of the Spotsylvania County militia and, during the War of 1812, was commissioned a Brigadier General. In 1793, Minor married his second wife, Lucy Landon Carter, with whom they had seven children. John Minor was a devoted family man and took pride in his children. Minor distinguished himself as a vocal opponent of slavery and freed his slaves and paid for their return to Liberia.

Minor was also involved in politics, serving for a time in the Virginia House of Burgesses. In 1816, Minor was a member of Virginia's Electoral College and had traveled from Fredericksburg to Richmond to cast his vote for the re-election of his friend President

All that remains of Hazel Hill is a historical marker on Princess Anne Street in Fredericksburg.

James Monroe.   On the night of June 8, 1816, Minor attended a dinner given in honor of the Electoral College by the citizens of Richmond. John Minor was in the process of giving a speech when he died suddenly from a stroke. Back in Fredericksburg, John Minor's family were preparing for dinner, unaware of the tragedy that had befallen them. Yet, according to Minor's children, in their father's last moments, his spirit returned one last time to the family and home that he loved.

The story was recorded a hundred years later by John Minor's granddaughter Mary Isabella Blackford. "My mother (Mary Minor Blackford) never did tell me this ghost story at all. I never heard it till after I was grown...My grandmother [Lucy Minor] had kept it a dead secret forty years. The servants had strict orders, not to mention it in Fredericksburg or anywhere. In those days, servants had to mind. As far as I know, they never did tell it," Blackford wrote.   It is unclear why Lucy Minor prevented her servants from discussing what may have happened at Hazel Hill the night John Minor died.

Though Lucy Minor and Mary Blackford never discussed the ghost sighting, an account of what happened was passed down to Mary Isabella through interviews with her uncles who were also at Hazel Hill that night. Mary Isabella recorded the story for her nephew Berkeley Minor. According to Mary Isabella:

"General Minor was at that time a member of the General Assembly that was meeting in Richmond.   My grandmother was not expecting him at all. She was sitting in her dining room at Hazle (sic.) Hill about 6 o'clock that evening...with her sons, their tutor and my mother, when suddenly the door opened and the butler, an elderly colored man, came in and said, 'Mistress, did you know Master had come?' She rose from the table quite excited and said, 'No, Ben, I was not expecting General Minor. Where is he?'

"Then they all followed Ben out in the hall and saw [General John Minor] at the lower end and just about to go upstairs. He turned a moment and looked at them and then went on up. He was in full evening dress. They could see his hand on the banister as he went up, and the ruffles at his wrist. Some went upstairs and searched every room, but he was nowhere to be found. The family were all excited and distressed, not knowing what to think."

Several hours later, a messenger arrived at Hazel Hill from Richmond with a letter detailing John Minor's death.   The sudden death of John Minor came as a shock to his friends and family. Though he had been ill in the days leading up to his death, he appeared to have recovered on the day he died. "On Thursday last at 1 o'clock, he was in the (Chancery) court, in better health and spirits than he usually enjoyed for some time past: a slight indisposition admonished him

The grave of John Minor and Lucy Minor in the Fredericksburg Masonic Cemetery on Caroline Street.

to retire to his lodgings; the symptoms becoming more violent, medical aid was called in; but the case was not considered as dangerous, on 12 o'clock of Saturday. On the evening of that day he thought himself much better, and seemed to be cheered by the circumstances of his pains having left him," an anonymous friend recorded in John Minor's obituary.

Like any great ghost story, there is also another version of the sighting of John Minor that was recorded by Minor's descendent Charles M. Blackford:

"In regard to the death of General Minor there is retained in the family a well authenticated incident which almost amounts to a ghost story. He died in Richmond...about eleven o'clock at night in the State capitol. The same evening there were assembled around the parlor fire at Cleve, in King George county (sic.), a number of the members of his wife's family, among them her brother-in-law, Mr. Wm. McFarland, a lawyer of talents, but more given to poetry than to law. He had a mind which would be called 'impressionable,' and which would make a good 'medium.' About eleven o'clock he left the room to go to bed, but in a moment returned somewhat alarmed, saying that he had seen General Minor in the gallery up stairs (sic.)–yet he was sure it was only his ghost. He was laughed at and told it was only his fancy, so he started out again, but returned with the same story, and then the whole went with him, but not being impressionable, the ghost was not seen. In a few days they learned that the time Mr. McFarland went up stairs was the hour at which General Minor had died in Richmond. Mr. McFarland's fancies ever afterwards were more esteemed. Of course, there was no ghost, nor was there anything supernatural in McFarland's vision. The art of photography and wireless telegraphy in the physical world prepares us to believe that on a mind peculiarly sensitive, impressions may be made by physical facts at a distance, to which the common mind is absolutely oblivious."

John Minor's earthly remains were returned to Fredericksburg, along with the route county courts that were in session adjourned out of respect. Following his funeral at St. George's Episcopal Church, Minor was buried at the family burial ground at Hazel Hill. In 1855 the remains of John Minor and his wife were reinterred in the Fredericksburg Masonic Cemetery.

In the mid-19th-century, the Minor family sold Hazel Hill, and the house would pass through several owners. The legacy of the sighting of John Minor's ghost remained with the house. In 1954, when family historian L. Minor Blackford visited Fredericksburg while writing a biography of Mary Minor Blackford, he was shocked to learn that Hazel Hill was known as "the old haunted house." Though he was dismayed that he "could find no one who knew why." Sadly, Hazel Hill no longer stands, but its memory lives on due in part to a ghostly sighting that occurred on the night John Minor died.

Donna Chasen, "Hazel Hill: Splendor of the Past," *Fredericksburg Free Lance Star*, August 14, 2004, https://www.fredericksburg.com/town_and_countylocal_history/hazel-hill-splendor-of-the-past/article_e8d98ace-13d1-58cd-9985-1cc8fb689611.html. (Accessed February 4, 2020).

"John Minor," Wythepedia: The George Wythe Encyclopedia, https://lawlibrary.wm.edu/wythepedia.php/John_Minor. (Accessed February 4, 2020).

"Brig. Gen. John Minor N-32," Fredericksburg, Stafford, Spotsylvania Historical Markers, fredmarkers.umwblogs.org/2008/03/23/brig-gen-john-minor-n-32/. (Accessed February 4, 2020).

Charles M. Blackford, "Four Successive John Minors (Concluded)," *The Virginia Magazine of History and Biography*, Vol. 10, N. 4 (Apr., 1903), 436.

L. Minor Blackford, *Mine Eyes Have Seen the Glory* (Cambridge, MA: Harvard University Press, 1954),

Richmond Enquirer, Richmond, VA, June 12, 1816, pg. 3.

"WEDGED INTO AN APPLE BIN" THE LINDEN MURDERS

Troy Taylor

$5,000 REWARD!

Murder!

TWO WOMEN AND ONE MAN BRUTALLY MURDERED.

On the afternoon of March 11th, 1924, at the hamlet Linden, on the Erie Railroad, in the Town of Bethany, Genesee County, N.Y., between the hours of 5:30 and 7 o'clock, Thomas Whaley, Hattie Whaley his wife, and Mrs. Mabel Morse, the wife of George Morse of Linden, New York, were murdered in the home of Thomas Whaley by an unknown person or persons. Mr. and Mrs. Whaley were both shot to death and Mrs. Morse was beaten to death. The pocketbooks of the victims were found rifled in the house.

Mrs. Morse wore a large open faced gold wrist watch with a gold chain bracelet attached. This is gone. Search all pawn shops for wrist watch.

Mr. Whaley's watch is also missing. It is a silver watch, heavy hunting case. Elgin movement No. 5,540,631, 15-jewel watch size 18. Case badly worn, as it had been carried by Mr. Whaley for 30 years.

The bodies of the victims were all dragged into a bedroom and covered with rugs and set on fire after being saturated with kerosene oil.

The County of Genesee offers a reward of $5,000 for information leading to the arrest and conviction of the person or persons guilty of the murder of Thomas Whaley, Mrs. Thomas Whaley and Mrs. Mabel Morse.

Address all communications to

HENRY W. WARE, Sheriff of Genesee County,

On November 12, 1917, the body of an unknown woman was discovered on some wooded property outside of the village of Linden, New York. Her identity was unknown - and so was that of her killer. It became the first in a series of horrific murders that remain unsolved.

Today, there is little left of the community of Linden, located about 40 miles from Buffalo. It's now just a cluster of houses, hidden away in the hills of southern Genesee County in New York. In the 1910s, though, Linden was a small farming town with about 100 residents who lived and worked on the surrounded acres. There was a post office back then, along with a general store, a railway station, a mill, and a blacksmith shop. Everyone knew one another - they'd been born and raised together. One person's business soon became everyone else's. There were few secrets among the friends, relatives, and neighbors of Linden. Perhaps this was why, when the murders began, the little community was so terrified. There was a killer among them - perhaps even someone they knew.

The first person to fall victim to the Linden killer was an unknown young woman, who was murdered on November 12, 1917. Her body was found in a wooded area of a farmer's property outside of town. Late on that chilly fall morning, the young woman, who was perhaps between 25 and 30 years old, was seen walking up a road that led into the woods. Witnesses later reported that she was wearing a black plush coat. There was a man walking with her. A short time later, the man was seen walking out of the woods - alone.

Three days later, Frank Hunt, the farmer who owned the property, found her body in the underbrush while gathering kindling for his heating stove. When he kicked aside some loose leaves and branches, he saw the woman's beaten, battered, and bloody face. She had been so disfigured that she barely looked human. The police were called to the scene, but they never identified the girl, and they never made any arrests. For lack of a better name, they called the mystery woman "Ruth."

The town was shocked to its core, but no one knew the girl. It was a mystery but such a strange occurrence that it just didn't shake people in the way that it could have. Such things didn't happen within their community. A stranger had been killed, but she must have brought the trouble with her. It was sad but soon forgotten. Life in the little farm town moved on.

But terror returned five years later.

On October 17, 1922, the killer claimed a second victim, and this time, it was someone that almost everyone in Linden knew. She was no stranger. She was a 73-year-old spinster named

The Kimball Farm off Linden Road

Frances Lenora Kimball

Frances Lenora Kimball, a feisty old woman who was best-known for her feelings against alcohol consumption and her support for the Prohibition laws that had banned alcohol in America. The hard-working, deeply religious woman grew apples and sold milk and eggs at her 60-acre farm off Linden Road near Skates Hill Road.

Miss Kimball's body was found hidden in the dark cellar of her home. Like the mysterious "Ruth," her head had been bashed in. The alarm over Miss Kimball's absence was first raised by her closest neighbor, Charles Speed, who stopped at her house that morning around 8:00 a.m. Her door was locked, and no one appeared to be about. He returned an hour later, knocked again, and received no answer. He realized soon after that, her cow had not been milked, which was something she did each day faithfully by 6:00 a.m., and he became alarmed. He told his wife, who called Miss Kimball's best friend, Miss Grace Smith, who, along with Mrs. Robert McWithey, went to the home. They had a key to the house but looked around and failed to find her. She was not in the barn either. The place seemed deserted. Miss Smith called Justice Maurice Nelan, the local magistrate, but his search of the property offered no clues - until he found that the telephone line had been cut. It was time to call the state police. Officers arrived and began scouring the entire property.

During a search of the cellar, State Police Corporal White illuminated a dark area with his flashlight and saw the body of Miss Kimball stuffed under a shelf, covered with an old door. Her head had been smashed in with a heavy object. The *Batavia Daily News* gave a gruesome account of the discovery:

Wedged into an empty apple bin, lying on her side, terribly disfigured, her brains protruding, her cheek bones broken, the body of the aged woman presented a spectacle to haunt the dreams of the most stone-hearted for many a night to come.

The newspaper's crime reporter called Miss Kimball, "the manifest object of the pent-up and deliberate fury of the animal's blows."

An autopsy showed that Miss Kimball had been hit about 20 times on the right side of her head with a heavy instrument. The beating had been so savage that fragments of her false teeth were found scattered all over the cellar floor. Semen was found on her clothing. The time of her death was established to be about 6:00 p.m. on the previous evening. Percy Fleming, a Linden resident, had seen her in the yard at 5:30 p.m., as he passed by the home.

After the discovery of the corpse by the state troopers, the local sheriff, district attorney, and coroner were summoned to the scene. The bulk of the investigation was turned over to William Doyle of the Doyle Detective Agency in Rochester, New York. In those days, with most police departments - especially in rural areas - ill-equipped to handle murder investigations, private detective agencies were often retained to carry out the investigations. Detectives, along with state troopers, questioned everyone who lived within a mile of the crime scene, including Miss Kimball's two elderly brothers, who had been away picking apples at the time of the murder.

The *Batavia Daily News* offered a $100 reward for information leading to the arrest of the killer. On October 21, Carl Meyers, a cousin of the dead woman, found a sharp, pointed rock with dried blood and gray hair on it in the corner of the cellar. The coroner determined that it had been the murder weapon. Detectives believe that whoever the killer was, he was familiar with the layout of the house. After the murder, he had locked all the doors and windows, including the front door, which he bolted when he left.

The police and detectives had no clues and no way to trace the killer. However, a local newspaper reported one detail that apparently came from an eyewitness but was not mentioned in later accounts of the crime: "Late on Monday evening, an automobile was driven into the Kimball farm and stood for a short time among the trees." There is no mention of the car ever being identified or of it being linked to anyone in the area, but it does become important in later theories about the case.

As the case stalled, the County of Genesee Board of Supervisors posted a reward of $1,000 for information leading to an arrest. But no one stepped forward to identify the killer. Whoever he was, he vanished without a trace -- again.

But the murders were far from over. The worse was still to come.

Seventeen months later, on March 11, 1924, three more Linden residents

Thomas and Hattie Whaley

Morse in the head. The killer put their bodies in a pile, covered them with old rugs, and set the rugs on fire. Neighbors found the bodies after breaking into the house to put out the flames. The fire, investigators believed, had been started to try and cover up the crime.

Thomas Whaley, 65, had worked for many years as a section boss on the Erie Railroad. His wife, Hattie, was 58, and neither of them was known to have any enemies. Mrs. Morse, 51, had stopped by the Whaley house to get some milk and visit with her friend, a regular thing for her to do. She had evidently surprised the killer at work. According to the autopsy, Mrs. Morse had been clubbed to death, and the Whaleys had both been shot by a .32-caliber revolver. The fire had been discovered by Myron Smith, a young man who was employed at the Morse store. When he arrived at the house, his quick actions kept the flames from spreading. The bodies had been blackened, and some of their clothing had been scorched away, but they were not burned beyond recognition. A few neighbors who rushed to the scene managed to use

were brutally slain. Thomas and Hattie Whaley lived in a home in the center of the village. That afternoon, Mable Morse, the wife of the proprietor of the general store, left to visit their home. When Mrs. Morse had not returned by the time her favorite radio program came on the air, one of her employees went to look for her. When he arrived at the Whaley house, he found it on fire. When the flames were put out, a gruesome discovery was made.

The newspapers of the day provided lurid details of the crime - and they immediately linked it to the Kimball murder of the previous year. The link to "Ruth" would not be made until much later.

The killer - called "a maniac" by the Buffalo newspaper - had shot both Whaleys and repeatedly struck Mrs.

pails of water to put out the fire before the house was too badly damaged.

Mrs. Morse had left the general store for the Whaley home at about 6:30 p.m., taking her milk pail with her. The Whaleys had a dairy cow and provided Mrs. Morse with milk each day. She was gone longer than usual. Usually, each evening, a group of people from the town gathered at the store to listen to a favorite radio program, which Mrs. Morse never missed. Fearing that she would not return in time for the show, Myron Smith hurried over to the Whaley home to remind her that it was about to start. He was joined by a friend, Milton Kettle, who worked with Mr. Whaley on the railroad.

Smith knew that Mr. Whaley had been ill for several days and thought Mrs. Morse might have stayed at the house to help out. He knocked on the door when he arrived, but no one answered. Oddly, he noticed that all the curtains on the windows had been drawn. After calling out, he tried the door and found it locked. Peering into the house, he saw smoke billowing about inside. He and Milton Kettle broke the window rear kitchen door and hurried inside. They were filled with horror when they saw the burned bodies stacked on the floor and covered with smoldering rugs. The young men rushed from the house and spread the alarm. In a matter of minutes, friends and neighbors had put out the fire and put in a call to state troopers in Batavia.

When the authorities arrived, they deduced that the Whaleys and Mrs. Morse had been killed, or nearly killed, in other rooms and then dragged into the front room, where they were finished off with the handle of a pick-ax. The later autopsy would show that Thomas Whaley had been shot in the neck. His wife had sustained a single gunshot wound to her head. Mrs. Morse had been clubbed to death with the wooden handle. Paper, bed clothing, and rugs were then wrapped around the bodies and saturated in kerosene oil, which came from a can found in the house. The killer's intention had been for the entire house to burn down, taking the bodies and all the evidence with it. He had closed all the curtains - even going as far as to nail a piece of cloth over one window that was not covered - so that he would not be seen. When he left the house, he locked all the doors to prevent the fire from being discovered. If not for the arrival of Milton and Kettle, his plan likely would have succeeded.

The newspapers were quick to point out that the circumstances in the Whaley-Morse murders were very similar to those in the murder of Frances Kimball in 1922 and also to the strange effort to burn down the home of Justice of the Peace Maurice Nelan, which adjoined the Kimball home, on September 23, 1923.

The investigation became heated at once. George Morse offered a $1,000 reward for the capture of the murderer of his wife, and the authorities swarmed over the village, where the Whaleys had been well-liked. Several tramps, a common sight along the railroad in Linden, were questioned. Linden was overrun by police -- the Genesee County Sheriff's Department and the fairly-new New York State Police shared the investigation -- by reporters from throughout Western New York, and even by sightseers who clogged the narrow, snow-covered roads.

Buffalo Police Captain Joseph Whitwell, chief of the Bertillon Bureau and a noted fingerprint expert at a time when the science was just taking hold in America, was retained and examined the scene. Unfortunately, though, fingerprints were of little value since the house had been so badly damaged by water from putting out the fire. Some believed that the murders were the result of a robbery since purses had been emptied, and watches and cash were missing. Others thought it was a maniac who had traveled along the railroad line. As the investigation proceeded, police became more convinced that the murderer was a local resident and concentrated their efforts around the community. No one was allowed to leave the area unless first checked by the police.

But as word spread about the murders, curiosity-seekers from Batavia, Rochester, and Buffalo swarmed to the area, impeding the investigation by causing traffic jams on the local roads. Local residents were questioned and then questioned again, but no solid leads ever developed. The state police kept a constant presence in Linden with one trooper assigned to stay in town, available for immediate duty, and two others on horses patrolling the surrounding area. The police were so desperate that when it was suggested that a picture of the murdered victim's eyes be taken with the belief that an image of the killer would be imprinted on the eyeball as the last vision of the victim, the photographs were taken. Needless to say, it didn't work, even though several newspapers claimed that the methods had been used to solve several important criminal cases.

Again, as in the Kimball murder, time passed, and the case grew cold. The few leads that the police obtained went nowhere, but interest in the case remained high -- and people were increasingly frightened. The available rewards grew larger. In addition to Mrs. Morse's offer of $1,000, the Genesee Board of Supervisors passed a resolution to offer $5,000 to the person furnishing information leading to the arrest and conviction of the slayers. With funds coming in from newspapers and other sources, the reward total eventually climbed to $8,000. Pleas for information were broadcast over the radio, but no substantial leads appeared.

And with so many cases that received wide attention, crackpots and kooks came looking for a moment in the spotlight. In March 1924, John Vetosky, who had been recently released from the Dannemora State Hospital for the Criminal Insane, confessed to the Linden slayings. He apparently gave a reasonable account of how he committed the crimes, but he later recanted, and his alibi was confirmed. A few of the investigators continued to believe that he was involved, but with a solid alibi, he could not be linked to any of the murders.

Later that summer, Linden Postmaster Ira J. Page Saturday received an anonymous letter from 'A Friend" that was postmarked Detroit, Michigan. The letter asked him to warn the village of an impending fifth murder, which was then being planned. It urged the postmaster to notify the authorities to be on their guard and to "watch and pray." Unfortunately, it was not the only letter to be sent, but like the warning of a "fifth murder," none of them amounted to anything.

In time, the frenzy calmed down, and the newspaper headlines became smaller. If there were any clear connections between the murder of the unknown woman in 1917, the Kimball murder of 1922, and the triple slayings of 1924, they were never discovered.

Linden, New York today

Over time, they became known as the "unsolved Linden murders." No one was ever arrested for any of the five murders. No motive was ever found, nor was the identity of the murderer or murderers ever determined. Gruesome and perplexing as they were, the Linden murders soon faded from the public's memory.

The story was later revived by author Rob R. Thompson who, with help from a retired FBI agent, took a new look at the old evidence and came to believe that he had figured out the identity of the killer.

Thompson, a former mental health counselor, began delving into the murders several years ago, going through thousands of pages of police reports, including the private notes left behind by investigators on the case. He was assisted in his research by Mark E. Safarik, a retired FBI agent and former violent crime analyst at the FBI

Academy. They came to the conclusion that the most viable suspect in the murders was a man named Andrew Michel.

According to Thompson, Michel died at the age of 77 in a Rochester mental institution in 1960. Although newspaper reports state that he was questioned by the police several times about the murders, he was never charged. There was also no physical evidence that linked Michel to the crimes. However, at the time of the murders, Michel lived in Linden near Miss Kimball and the Whaleys. He had worked on local farms as a hired hand and had also worked at a steel plant and on the railroad. Shortly after the Whaley-Morse murders, he moved away from Linden to nearby Attica.

Thompson came up with some compelling reasons that suggest he may be right about Michel being the killer, namely that he had grudges against Kimball, the Whaleys, and Mrs. Morse. Kimball, an advocate against liquor, had reported Michel for illegally making hard cider. Months before she was killed, she had argued with Michel over the drinking habits of her brother, William Kimball. She had also appeared as a witness against him in an animal cruelty case. Michel had been fined $25 after he was accused of beating a horse with a piece of wood so violently that one of the horse's eyes had been knocked out. Locals knew he had a violent streak.

According to the investigator's notes, Thomas Whaley had identified Michel as a suspect in a 1923 arson case. He had also refused to lend Michel money, and Mrs. Whaley had once told a neighbor that she suspected that Michel had killed Miss Kimball.

Whaley's anger with the Morse family was caused by money problems. Two weeks before the murders at the Whaley home, George Morse had sent Michel a letter, cutting off his credit at the general store until he paid off a debt of $160.

Michel had never been silent about his dislike of Miss Kimball or the Whaleys and Morses. While he repeatedly told the police that he had nothing to with the murders, a man named Brad Burroughs told detectives that he once heard Michel make angry threats to kill Kimball, someone from the Morse family and others in 1916 -- vowing that he would kill them if it took 10 or 15 years to do it.

There were others who had run-ins with Michel, including Justice of the Peace Nelan, who were later shocked when serious arson fires were started on their property. Witnesses, including Thomas Whaley, told police they saw Michel leaving the Nelan fire scene, but he was never charged with any arson.

According to Thompson, Michel worked clearing wood in the area where the mystery woman's body was found in 1917, which may link him to that crime, as well.

But the police never charged Michel with any of the murders. Twelve days after the Whaley-Morse murders, police told the Buffalo newspaper that Michel had been "freed of suspicion" after lengthy questioning. At that time, a detective noted that the right-handed Michel had only one finger on his right hand because of a sawmill accident that occurred when he was young. That one finger was "twice the size of an ordinary finger" and would not fit into the trigger guard of the type of handgun allegedly used to shoot the Whaleys, the detective stated. But was this really enough to rule him out? The victims had been shot at close range, which could have been done with either hand. Michel also had a tendency to use a wooden club, which had demonstrated on the unfortunate horse.

But not everyone is convinced by Thompson's theory. Michel is, of course, long dead and cannot defend himself. Court documents show that a petition was filed in Wyoming County Court in 1958, asking a judge to declare Michel mentally incompetent. Two years later, he died in a Rochester mental hospital. So, if he was the killer, the secret of the murders died with him. And with everyone else involved the case long since dead, there can be no conclusive answers.

Some believe the killer may have come from the Genesee County Poor House, which is now called Rolling Hills Asylum

But even today, theories remain. It's been suggested that the murders were committed by "a transient" -- someone who occasionally passed through Linden, perhaps hopping rides on freight trains. Police did question several "vagrants," but never charged any of them. Others have suggested that the murders were committed by a deranged person who lived at the old Genesee County Poor House, a building that once housed the poor, the elderly, and some mental patients who could not fend for themselves. Now known as Rolling Hills Asylum - and believed to be haunted - the poor house closed in the 1970s and was not far from the murders.

The mystery remains, and the Linden Murders are still officially unsolved.

"THE MOST HAUNTED HOUSE IN AMERICA"

I'll never forget the first time that I read about the "Most Haunted House in America" - mostly because it scared the crap out of me. I was around 11- or 12-years-old, and it soon became one of my favorite tales of ghosts, horror, and the supernatural. It chilled me to the bone, and I seriously never doubted that the story must be true. In the years that followed, my interest in the story never faded, and as time passed, I should have realized that something was not quite right about it, but I never did. Or perhaps I just didn't want to see it.

The story of the "Most Haunted House in America" seemed too good to be true - simply because it was.

I wasn't the only one who was fooled by the story, but I'm

THE INFAMOUS GHOST STORY THAT WASN'T

Troy Taylor

The 1100 Block of Ridge Avenue in the early 1900s. The REAL 1129 Ridge Avenue "mansion" is at the corner. As you can see, it looks nothing like the depictions of the "Congelier Mansion" that have been floating around since the 1990s

embarrassed to say that when I look back now, I don't understand how I missed the signs. When I finally began to accept the idea that the story had a lot of issues, I became determined to track down all the facts - and soon ran into problems.

As I began contacting people who should have been aware of the details of a story that took place in Pittsburgh, Pennsylvania, I quickly realized that those who claimed knowledge about the house, which was allegedly located on Ridge Avenue, were simply repeating back to me the same story that I'd already heard. They cited the same sources, and as far as I can tell, this "local legend" first appeared in the book *Haunted Houses* by Richard Winer and Nancy Osborn. I have never been able to find out where they heard

the story, and to this day, I have no idea who started it.

My search led in circles. The same story was regurgitated back to me over and over again. People who claimed to recall the details behind the events suddenly forgot them, and witnesses who stated that they had information that went beyond the standard accounts became bewildered when the story did not match the historical details of the case.

This is not my first article about the "House on Ridge Avenue" - and it may not be my last - but I have discovered more of the details behind the legend than I've ever known before. I think you'll enjoy the story - and the truth behind the story, too.

Believe me when I tell you that the "legend" and the "truth" are two very

Mary Cancelliere's five children, left motherless by the Equitable Gas Company explosion.

Pittsburgh Press, November 16, 1927

different things when it comes to this house.

The House on Ridge Avenue

On November 14, 1927, storage tanks along the Ohio River that belonged to the Equitable Gas Company exploded on Pittsburgh's North Side. The blast did significant damage to several blocks of homes of businesses, and 28 people were killed, including a young mother named Mary Cancelliere.

Mary's death was a freak accident. A window in the laundry room of her home shattered, and she was struck by flying glass. Her death at the age of only 29 was tragic enough, but she also left five young children behind.

The unusual nature of Mary's death, combined with the long and shadowy history of her family's connections to organized crime in Pittsburgh, would spawn an urban legend in the 1970s that earned her home on Ridge Avenue widespread fame in the supernatural community. Whether it deserved it or not.

The Legend: Part 1

According to the legend, the House on Ridge Avenue was located in a quiet residential neighborhood in Manchester, on the north edge of Pittsburgh. A man named Charles Wright Congelier built it in the 1860s. He had made a fortune for himself in Texas following the Civil War, and such men were commonly referred to in the south as "Carpetbaggers." They made a lot of money preying on the broken economy in the former Confederacy. Congelier left Texas by river steamer, taking with him his Mexican wife, Lyda, and a servant girl named Essie. When the steamer docked in Pittsburgh for coal, Congelier decided that the Pennsylvania town looked like a good place to settle. The three of them left the ship, and Congelier purchased a lot and began construction of the house.

A few months later, the new brick and mortar mansion was completed. It was located at 1129 Ridge Avenue and was considered one of the finest houses in the area. From the expansive lawn, Congelier could look out and see where the Allegheny and Monongahela Rivers met the Ohio River, offering a breathtaking view. The former Carpetbagger soon became a respected member of the local business community, and his new home became a frequent site for parties and social gatherings. Then, during the winter of 1871, an event took place that would bloody the location for decades to come.

That winter, as cold and snow settled over the region, Congelier became embroiled in an affair with his servant girl, Essie. Whether she was a willing participant or not, Essie soon became a constant bed partner for her employer. For several months, Lyda Congelier was unaware of the affair, but when three people reside in the same house, it's only a matter of time before secrets are revealed.

One afternoon, Lyda returned from a shopping trip and needed the girl to help her with her packages. She came into the house, but Essie was nowhere to be found. When Essie did not respond to her call, Lyda went to the

Popular depiction of a "Carpetbagger," taking advantage of the poor and disenfranchised in the South after the Civil War. There were not popular with former residents of the Confederacy.

girl's room looking for her. As she came down the hallway, she could hear heavy breathing and moaning coming from behind the door. Knowing that her husband was the only man in the house, Lyda became enraged. She hurried to the kitchen and snatched up both a butcher knife and a meat cleaver. As she began climbing the stairs back to the servant's room, Lyda began screaming with rage, which naturally provoked a panic inside of Essie's bedroom. Before Congelier and the girl could get dressed and exit the room, Lyda had already taken up a post outside. When the door opened, she brought the meat cleaver down on the

head of the first person to open it. Charles Congelier fell to the floor, a cry on his lips and blood streaming from the wound on his head. As Essie reared back, bellowing in terror, Lyda proceeded to stab her husband 30 times. Then, she turned her wrath on Essie.

Several days later, a family friend called at the house, and when no one responded to his knock, he opened the door and peered inside. He called out, but there was no answer in the darkened house. However, as he entered the foyer, he could hear a faint creaking noise in the parlor. He called out again, but when there was still no answer, he walked further into the house. Following the odd sound, he entered the parlor and saw Lyda Congelier rocking back and forth in front of a large bay window. The wooden chair that she rested in creaked with each backward and forward motion that she made.

"Lyda? Is everything all right?" he spoke to her.

There was no reply. Lyda continued to rock back and forth in the chair. As her friend drew closer, he could hear her softly crooning a lullaby under her breath. It was a child's nursery song, he realized, and he saw a bundle that was wrapped in a blanket in Lyda's arms. She held it close, as she would hold a baby, rocking it gently. The man felt a sudden chill course through him. He knew that the Congelier's had no children.

He spoke to her once again, but there was still no answer. Lyda stared straight ahead through the window, her eyes glazed and unfocused. He gently leaned over and eased the bundle out of her hands. He carefully opened the pink blanket and then recoiled with horror, dropping the bloody bundle onto the floor. It landed on the wooden floorboards with a solid thud, and the contents of the blanket rolled away.

The friend fell backward on the couch as Essie's bloody head came to a halt a short distance away from his feet.

For more than two decades after, the house on Ridge Avenue remained empty. Local folks considered the place "tainted" and avoided it at all costs. Few dared to even trespass on the grounds, although sometimes small children threw stones at the windows and sang about the "old battle-ax and her meat-ax."

The Real Story: Part 1

Like most legends, the story of the house is a clever blending of fact and fiction, although in this case, there is much more fiction than fact. To start with, no one named Charles Wright Congelier ever existed, and neither did his wife, Lyda. There is no record of any dealings in Texas and no record of him ever living in Pittsburgh. In addition, there are no police or criminal records that state that Lyda murdered her husband and the servant girl in 1871. The use of a date here adds depth to the story, but it also makes it easier to check the validity of the tale. In this case, there isn't any.

Secondly, the house that is described in the story didn't exist. There were no mansions in that neighborhood. The real house located at 1129 Ridge Avenue was a narrow, eight-room Manchester row house, a common, working-class home of the late nineteenth century.

Charles Wright Congelier, and the murderous Lyda, were figments of creative imagination - conjured up by mistake. It was derived from the misspelled "Cancelliere" name that was published in newspapers after the explosion in 1927.

The Legend: Part 2

In 1892, the house was renovated into an apartment building to house railroad workers. Most refused to stay in the place for long. They constantly complained of hearing screams and the sobbing of a woman that came from empty rooms. Others spoke of the ominous sounds of a rocking chair and of a woman mumbling old nursery rhymes and lullabies. Within two years, the house was abandoned once again.

It remained vacant until 1901 when Dr. Adolph C. Brunrichter purchased the house. The doctor became something of an enigma in the neighborhood. Although he received warnings about the history of the house, he ignored them and, after moving in, had little to do with the neighbors. He kept to himself and was rarely seen by those who lived nearby. Everyone in the neighborhood watched and held their breath, waiting for something terrible to happen.

They didn't have to wait long.

On August 12, 1901, the family who lived next door to the Brunrichter mansion heard a terrifying scream coming from the house. When they ran outside to see what was going on, they saw a bright red flash illuminate the interior of the mansion. The windows

of the house shattered, and glass shot outward onto the lawn. The air was filled with the smell of ozone, and the earth under the neighborhood trembled, cracking the sidewalks and knocking over furniture in the surrounding homes.

By the time that the police and the fire department arrived, a crowd had gathered outside of Brunrichter's house. It was assumed that the doctor was still inside -- no one had seen him leave -- but none of the neighbors were brave enough to go in and check. Finally, a contingent of firefighters entered the house in search of Brunrichter. They were unable to find him, but what they did discover was enough to send even the bravest among them running for the street outside.

In one of the upstairs bedrooms, a gut-wrenching scene awaited police investigators. Lying spread-eagled on the blood-soaked bed was the decomposing, naked body of a young woman. Her head was missing and was later found in a makeshift laboratory that the doctor had set up in another room. From what the detectives could determine, Brunrichter had apparently been experimenting with severed heads. Using electrical equipment, he had been trying to keep the heads alive after decapitation. A fault in his equipment had evidently caused the explosion. The young girl's head was found with several others, and the graves of five women were discovered in the cellar. Each of the bodies could be matched with one of the heads from the laboratory.

As for Dr. Brunrichter, there was no sign of him. He had apparently escaped during the confusion following the explosion and had vanished. A manhunt produced no clues. He had disappeared without leaving a trace.

In September 1927, an old man was arrested in New York's Bowery district. He was found wandering in a drunken stupor, living among the homeless and the street people. He was arrested and booked for public drunkenness and was taken to the local police station house. Standing in line with the other dirty and disheveled men, this particular vagrant seemed to give off what the officers would later recall as a "bad feeling." As the drunks shuffled along, the policemen entered their names into record one at a time. When the old man reached the head of the line, the officer asked him his name.

He replied in a harsh voice, slightly slurred with a foreign accent. "My name is Adolph Brunrichter," the man said. And soon, he began to tell stories of his life to the officers at the police station, and they were tales even the most hardened cops would not soon forget.

Brunrichter began by explaining to the officers that he was once an eminent doctor, a physician who worked diligently to prolong life. Unfortunately, he could only succeed with his experiments by ending the lives of certain test subjects. He told of how many years earlier, he had bought a house in Pittsburgh to which he enticed young women as guests. Anticipating romance, the women were instead beheaded and then used in experiments to keep their severed heads alive. Brunrichter told of sex orgies, torture, and murder and then gave the locations of graves for other women who were not discovered in the cellar of the house. Authorities later checked the sites, but no bodies were ever found.

Brunrichter was kept behind bars for one month at Blackwell's Island. Despite newspaper stories that called him the "Pittsburgh Spook Man," the mad doctor was deemed "harmless" and was released. On the wall of his cell, scrawled in his own blood, were the words "What Satan hath wrought, let man beware." After those ominous words, nothing was ever heard from the man who claimed to be Dr. Adolph Brunrichter again.

The Real Story: Part 2

The house was built in 1886 and, while a working-class home, was not used to house railroad workers. It was one of five brick houses that were built at the corner of Ridge Avenue and Sproat Alley. It had been constructed by John Jacob Lawrence, a Civil War veteran and paint company founder who had bought the property in the 1880s from the Allegheny Gas Works Company.

The house changed hands many times over the years, mostly being rented out until the early 1920s. In 1923, Julia T. Manning sold it to Jack Cancelliere - who we'll come back to soon.

At no time was the house ever owned by anyone named Dr. Adolph Brunrichter. Like Charles and Lyda Congelier, he never existed. The only mention of Brunrichter that I have ever been able to find in my own extensive files and books about American crime is in connection to this house. This seemed rather odd to me since his crimes certainly would have been gruesome and lurid enough to garner the attention of reporters and crime writers. However, there are no listings for him in any books that I could find.

Not content to let it go at that, I also contacted several noted crime researchers and asked them to check their own files for mentions or records of Brunrichter. None of them could find anything. Another check of newspaper and library archives for New York, where papers had allegedly written of the "Pittsburgh Spook Man," also failed to reveal any listings. The same problem occurred while trying to search for reports of the crimes in Pittsburgh, as well. There is no mention of the "explosion" or the discovery of the bodies in the house in the Pittsburgh newspapers. In addition, there is not a single death record, real estate record, or police record involving anyone named Brunrichter in connection with the house on Ridge Avenue.

The mysterious Dr. Brunrichter vanished without a trace because he never existed in the first place.

The Legend: Part 3

After the horrific discoveries in the basement of the house, the Ridge Avenue mansion was abandoned. It stood empty again for many years, gaining an even more fearsome reputation. Those with an interest in psychic phenomena made occasional visits to the place and came to believe that the house was inhabited by a "fearsome presence." One medium who investigated the house, Julia Murray, detected a horrible spirit there, and witnesses who accompanied her to the mansion stated that "objects hurled by unseen hands barely missed striking her." Murray predicted that the entity would kill and would eventually extend out beyond the confines of the house.

In 1920, the stories about the mansion caught the attention of another man, one of the greatest inventors that America has ever known. His name was Thomas Alva Edison, and in addition to creating the light bulb, he went to his grave in search of a device that would be able to communicate with the dead.

Edison was a self-taught genius who began experimenting with scientific theories as a child. Throughout his life, he maintained that it was possible to build anything if the right components were available. This would later include the machine that communicated with the dead. Edison was not a believer in the supernatural, however, nor a proponent of the popular Spiritualist movement. He had always been an agnostic, and although he did not dispute the philosophies of religion, he didn't necessarily believe in

(Left) Thomas Edison — who never visited the house at 1129 Ridge Avenue but somehow became part of the legend.

(Above) The Psycho Phone device that was not invented by Edison as a "machine to communicate with the dead." It was adapted from plans allegedly received from Edison's ghost during a séance.

their truth either. He believed that when a person died, the body decayed, but the intelligence the man possessed lived on. He thought that the so-called "spirit world" was simply a limbo where disembodied intelligence still existed. He took these paranormal theories one step further by announcing that he intended to devise a machine that could communicate with this "limbo." Edison's announcement appeared in newspapers after his visit to the house on Ridge Avenue. What happened during his visit to the house is unknown, but whatever it was, it certainly inspired him to go to great lengths to create the machine.

According to journals and papers, Edison began working on the apparatus. The famous magician and friend of Edison's, Joseph Dunninger, claimed that he was shown a prototype of the machine, but few others ever say they saw it. Edison reportedly continued working on the machine until his death in October 1931. Did Edison's machine exist? And if so, would it have worked? In the years following his death, curators at both Edison museums in Florida and New Jersey have searched extensively for the components, the prototype, or even the plans for the machine to communicate with the dead. So far, they have found nothing, making Edison's device the greatest mystery of his complex and intriguing life.

The Real Story: Part 3

In the best hoaxes, fact and fiction are blended using real dates and real people to create a convincing story. In the case of the House on Ridge Avenue, the names of people like Julia Murray and Thomas Edison have been used to make the story seem more real. Obviously, Edison really did exist, and he did attempt to create a machine to communicate with the dead, but unfortunately, no records exist of any spirit medium named Julia Murray.

I will not state definitively that she is a fictional character, but so far, I have found nothing that proves she was a real person - although I wonder if her name might have been invented from one of the owners of the house, Julia Manning. It's not exactly the same, but it's certainly close.

Edison, on the other hand, was very real, but there is absolutely no record to say that he ever set foot in the house on Ridge Avenue. If he had, he would not have found an empty "haunted" house, but the home of the Manning family.

The Legend: Part 4

In the middle 1920s, Julia Murray's premonitions of "evil" connected to the house on Ridge Avenue came back to haunt it. During this period, the Equitable Gas Company, which was located just a few blocks away, was nearing the completion of a huge natural gas storage complex. To cut costs, many of the regular workers were laid off and were replaced by Italian immigrants, who would work for a much lower wage. Several vacant buildings in the neighborhood were converted into apartments, including the house at 1129 Ridge Avenue.

The Italian workers who took up residence in the house quickly realized that something was not right in the old mansion. Their complaints and reports were met with quick explanations from the supervisors at the gas company. They told the immigrants that the strange occurrences were the work of the American workers who had been replaced. The former employees were playing tricks on the new workers, hoping they would abandon their jobs. The men soon dismissed the strange sounds and ghostly footsteps as practical jokes until an incident occurred a few months after they moved in.

One evening, 14 men were seated around the table in the common dining room. They had just finished consuming large quantities of pasta and were now laughing and talking over glasses of homemade wine. One of the men got up and carried a stack of dirty dishes into the kitchen. He joked to his brother as he left the room, calling out a humorous insult over his shoulder with a smile. The remark was answered with laughter, and his brother tossed a crust of bread at his sibling's retreating back. The conversation continued for several minutes before the remaining man realized that his brother had not returned from the kitchen. He got up and walked into the other room to find the door to the basement standing open.

Suddenly, the festive mood in the dining room was shattered by a chilling scream. Rushing into the kitchen, the men saw the open basement door. Taking a lantern from atop the icebox, several of the men descended the steps into the cellar. Before they reached the bottom of the steps, they froze, staring at the macabre scene that was illuminated by the glow of the lantern. In the dim light, they saw the man who had left the dining room just moments earlier, now hanging from a floor beam that crossed the ceiling above.

On the floor, directly beneath his feet, was the man's brother. He was lying face down in a spreading pool of blood. A splintered board had been driven through his chest and now exited out through his back.

The leader of the group on the steps crossed himself religiously, and a gasp escaped from his lips. His friends repeated the gesture before all of them found themselves slammed backward by a force that they could not see. The feeling of a cold wind pushed against them and then rushed up the stairs. The men later said that they could hear the pounding of footsteps on the wooden treads but could see nothing at all. The door at the top of the stairs slammed shut, startling the men still in the kitchen. Moments later, other doors began slamming throughout the house.

When the police arrived, they attributed both deaths to a bizarre accident. The first man, the detectives stated, tripped on a loose step and fell down, impaling himself on the propped-up board. The other brother's death was the result of the same loose stair step. When he fell, though, his head was somehow tangled on an electric wire that was hanging down above the staircase. Accident or not, the other men quickly moved out of the house, wanting nothing more to do with the place.

The Real Story: Part 4

Once again, real-life events blend into the story to make it more compelling. In the 1920s, the nearby Equitable Gas Company did lay off many of its workers and replaced them with Italian immigrants. As many of the houses in the neighborhood were worker's homes anyway, several of them were converted into housing for the replacement employees. The house at 1129 Ridge Avenue was not one of them, and there were no accidental deaths in the house during this time, especially those of temporary workers.

One accident did take place, however, on the same day that another accident destroyed a gas storage tank nearby.

On the morning of the explosion, Mary Cancelliere died from a laceration caused by a piece of glass. The glass severed her artery, and she bled to death on the way to the hospital. She did not die in the house, but her death came about because of it --- with nothing supernatural involved.

She would become the only death that can truly be connected to the House on Ridge Avenue.

On Monday, November 14, 1927, a crew of 16 workers climbed to the top of the Equitable Gas Company's huge, 5,000,000-cubic-foot natural gas storage tank to find and repair a leak.

At 8:43 that morning, a great sheet of flame erupted from the tank, and the huge container shot impossibly upwards into the air. Steel, stone, and human bodies were sent hurling into the sky. Two of the men who had been working on top of the tank were thrown against a brick building more than 100 feet away, and their silhouettes were outlined on the wall in blood. Seconds later, another tank exploded, creating another gigantic ball of fire. Then a third tank, this one only partially full, was wrenched apart and added to the inferno. Smoke and flames were visible for miles. The force was so tremendous that it blew out windows and shook buildings over a 25-mile radius. Locomotives were knocked over, and homes and structures were damaged as far away as East Liberty.

Across the street, the Union Paint Company was flattened, and dozens of workers were buried under the rubble of the building. Bloody men, women, and children ran frantically about in the streets.

The Battalion Chief of Engine Company No. 47, Dan Jones, was part of the first fire unit to arrive on the scene. He described the holocaust saying, "great waves of black smoke swept through the streets, and there was a whining noise in the air." According to a book compiled by the Writer's Project of America, the destruction stunned the city. "As houses collapsed and chimneys toppled, brick, broken glass, twisted pieces of steel, and other debris rained on the heads of the dazed and shaken residents who had rushed into the streets from their wrecked homes, believing that an earthquake had visited the city."

Several rescue workers and firefighters who arrived on the scene were injured and killed when weakened structures collapsed on top of them. Entire neighborhoods were flooded by broken water mains while huge sections of the city lay in ruins. Sections of the giant gas storage tanks were later found more than 1,000 feet away. Rough estimates created the following day, listed at least 28 killed

and more than 600 people injured from the explosion. Rescue crews dynamited the ruins in a search for the bodies of the dozens of others who were still missing. Thousands were left homeless by the destruction.

Mounds of rubble and debris marked the spots where buildings had once stood. At one place, though, not even bricks and stone remained. At 1129 Ridge Avenue, just two blocks away from the blast site, there was nothing left but a smoldering crater. Although homes on both sides of, and across the street from, where the Congelier mansion had stood were heavily damaged, they were still standing. Yet where the "most haunted house in America' had stood, and where Julia Murray's proclaimed "evil presence" had lingered, there was nothing. A hole that nearly 85-feet deep was all that remained. It was the only house in the vicinity of which no trace could be found.

Today, the Carnegie Science Center occupies the site of the Equitable Gas Company tanks, and the terrible explosion is only a faint memory from the past. The house on Ridge Avenue is all but forgotten. Its location is the present-day site of the Route 65 and Interstate 279 interchange. Nothing from the days of Dr. Brunrichter, the Congeliers, or the luckless Italian immigrants still lingers, or does it?

If it is possible for the spirits of the past to still wander restlessly along a busy highway, then it would be at this

Two Historic Pittsburgh photos showing the damage caused by the Equitable Gas Company explosion in 1927.

place where such spirits would dwell --- the place where one of the most evil houses in the country could be found.

The Real Story: Part 5

Spooky ending, right?

Unfortunately, it's not accurate either.

The gas storage tank at the Equitable Gas Company did explode on November 14, 1927 and killed 24 people in the surrounding area. The concussion and subsequent fire did wreak havoc in this part of the city, and it destroyed many houses and buildings, leaving hundreds of people homeless. The details of the destruction that are recounted in the legend of the house are true and accurate --- for the most part.

Of course, the story veers wildly into fiction when we get to the house at 1129 Ridge Avenue. In every version of the story, the house is destroyed by the blast, leaving only an ominous crater behind --- as if it were sucked down into the very pit of hell. While this makes a fitting ending to the dramatic tale of "America's most haunted house," it's not the way that it happened. In truth, the house only suffered minor damage from the explosion. The worst thing to occur was the shattering of several windows, glass from which took Mary Cancelliere's life.

The Real Story: The Cancellieres

As we have already established, no one named Congelier ever lived in the house at 1129 Ridge Avenue. It was not a mansion, but a narrow, eight-room, 21-foot-wide, two-and-half-story brick row house. The name "Congelier" came from a misspelling of "Cancelliere" in the newspaper after the explosion. And it didn't hurt that the Cancellieres already had some notoriety in Pittsburgh when the legend of their "haunted house" began.

Unlike the fictional Congelier, Mary and her husband, Giacomo "Jack" Cancelliere, didn't arrive in Pittsburgh after the Civil War. Before moving to the city, they had been living in the coalfields of Southwest Pennsylvania, where Jack worked as a miner. He had emigrated to America with his extended family from Villarosa, a town in Sicily. Mary was also from Villarosa and came to America with her father.

Pittsburgh mob hangout the Rosa Villa was owned by the Cancelliere family

Jack was nine years older than Mary when they were married in 1913. Their marriage license, as well as immigration records, census records, and land deeds, show where they lived during the first two decades of the twentieth century.

In 1923, they moved to Pittsburgh, and it was this same year that Jack was arrested for the first time for bootlegging. It would not be his last brush with the law. He also bought the house on Ridge Avenue from Julia

Bomb and arson squad detectives are investigating a blast, attributed to bombers, which wrecked the front of the home of Santo Laquatra, 1335 Page street, Northside, early yesterday, damaged two neighboring dwellings, and broke windows in buildings in the vicinity. Damage was estimated at $10,000. The Laquatra home is shown above, with the home of W. L. Cooley, 1333 Page street, to the left in the picture. The home of Mrs. Nellie Zickis, 1337 Page street, was the other house most severely damaged.

— Post Gazette Photo.

In 1932, the home of Santo Laquatra — where the Cancelliere children went to live after their mother was killed — was targeted by rival mobsters (Pittsburgh Press Photo)

Manning and put the title in Mary's name. This was a common tactic by organized crime figures so that their property could not be seized by law enforcement.

In January 1927, Jack also bought a three-story building at 106 East General Robinson Street that became the infamous Rosa Villa Restaurant.

Over the next 30 years, both 1129 Ridge Avenue and the Rosa Villa often appeared in newspaper articles about Jack or members of his extended family, who also lived in the house, being arrested - mostly for bootlegging and gambling. Law enforcement officials had thick files on the Cancellieres and the restaurant, which was widely known by local residents and cops as a popular mob hangout.

The house became notorious, too. In 1939, Angelo Cancelliere was indicted for assaulting a police officer who tried to arrest him. The address on his arrest record was 1129 Ridge Avenue, just as it was when he was arrested that same year for operating a lottery.

Violence surrounded multiple generations of the Cancelliere family for much of the twentieth century. After the Equitable Gas Company explosion, Mary's children went to live with her husband's family on nearby Page Street. That house was owned by Santo Laquatra, Jack's relative, and the person who sold him the Rosa Villa property. In 1932, that house was damaged during an organized crime turf war that led to bombings and murders across the city. The Rosa Villa itself, which was torn down in 2019, was targeted in a failed bombing attempt in 1958. The authorities linked it to a "racket war" that was going on at the time.

Historian and folklorist David S. Rotenstein believes that the 1927 gas explosion and rumors about one of Pittsburgh's best-known mid-twentieth-century racketeering families created the perfect circumstances for folks to spin wild stories about the house at 1129 Ridge Avenue. It became one of Pittsburgh's most enduring legends. He believes that the catastrophic explosion, combined with true organized crime history, created the perfect conditions for creating ghost stories -- a folk strategy for organizing fear and uncertainty and deflecting attention from sensitive subjects like death and crime.

And he's undoubtedly right, although I'd be curious to know who originally created the insane tale of the Congeliers, Dr. Brunrichter, and the ongoing theme of severed heads and extreme violence that permeates the tale. Whoever it was, they remain unknown, even though they helped create a cottage industry in Pittsburgh that has endured beyond my initial debunking of the story in 2003. It still appears in books and magazine and newspaper articles, and it's regularly featured on ghost tours that take visitors to Ridge Avenue to hear the legends recounted.

The house at 1129 Ridge Avenue was never the "most haunted house in America" by any stretch of the imagination. And it probably wasn't haunted, although we'll never know for sure since it was demolished in the late 1960s. It's now a parking lot.

It's often said that "truth is stranger than fiction." Most of the time, this is accurate, but not with every story. In the story of the House on Ridge Avenue, I'd have to say that fiction was definitely much stranger than fact could ever be.

Truth turned out to be the undoing of "America's Most Haunted House."

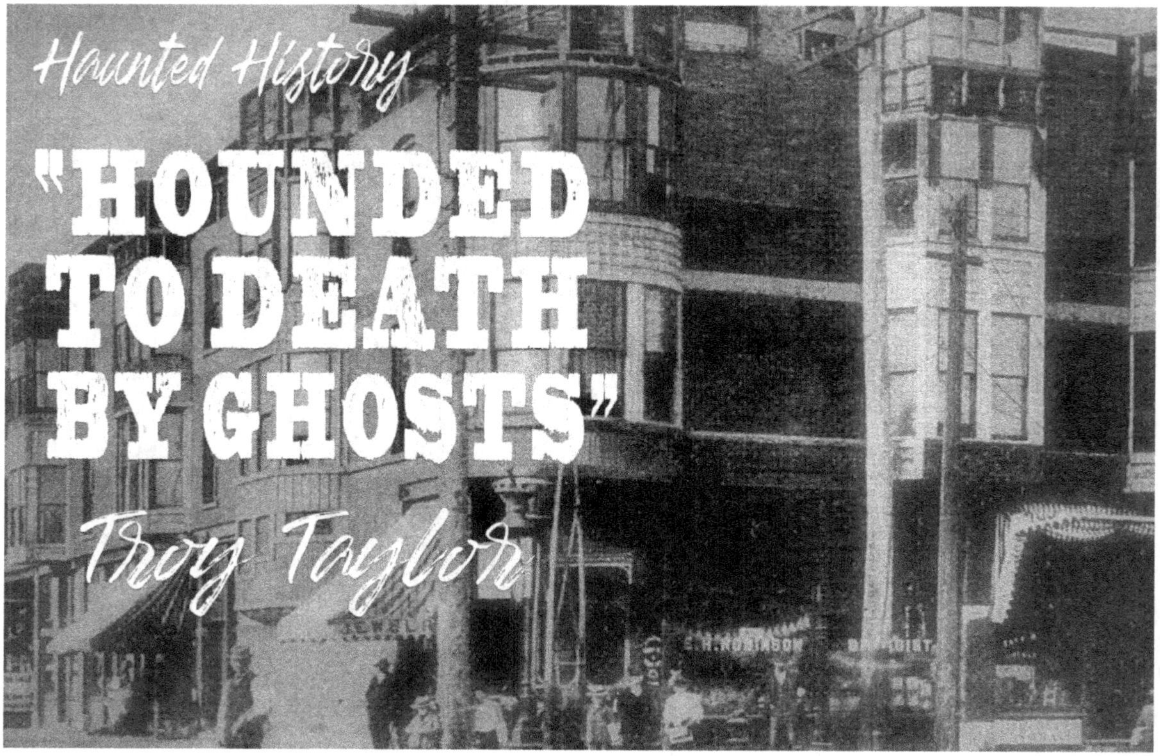

Haunted History

"HOUNDED TO DEATH BY GHOSTS"

Troy Taylor

THE STORY OF THE DEVIL'S ACCOMPLICE

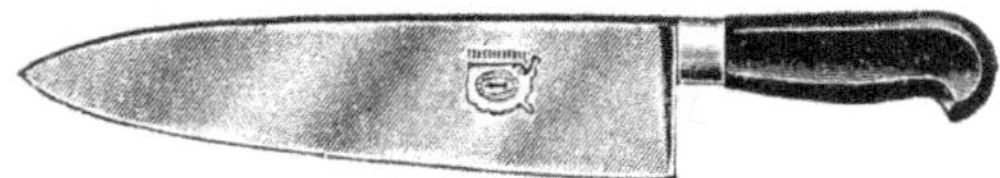

In 1914, the news of a man's suicide in the small town of Portland, Michigan, was barely noticed by the newspapers of the day. The man's name was Patrick Quinlan, a poor Irishman who mostly kept to himself. Even the strange circumstances of his death failed to attract any real attention. Quinlan had taken a fatal dose of poison and left a note lying on the floor next to his body. On the scrap of paper, he had scrawled just four words, "I could not sleep."

Few remembered Quinlan's claim to infamy as the accused accomplice of a man named H.H.

Holmes, one of the most prolific murderers in American history. Shortly after Holmes' arrest in 1895, Quinlan, who had worked as a janitor at Holmes' "Murder Castle" in Chicago, was also taken into police custody. He was soon released and forgotten, mentioned mostly as an afterthought in the myriad of writings that have since appeared about the murderous life of Holmes.

But was Patrick Quinlan really as innocent as the police said that he was? There were many who didn't believe so, including a man who claimed that he was almost murdered by him, neighbors who believed that he disposed of damning evidence --- and perhaps even Quinlan himself. What really led to his suicide? Guilt over what he had done while in the employ of Holmes, or was he, as some would later claim, hounded to his death by the ghosts of his victims?

H.H. Holmes remains one of the most notorious criminals in the history of America. He was an accomplished swindler, a specialist at insurance fraud, and an unrepentant murderer who killed dozens of people that we know of and may have also claimed many additional victims at his "Murder Castle" during the 1893 Columbian Exposition in Chicago. Holmes had arrived in Illinois a few years before the exposition, settling first in

Pat Quinlan's employer, Herman Mudgett, better known today as H.H. Holmes

Wilmette, and then moving to Englewood, where he "purchased" a profitable drug store from an elderly woman who disappeared soon after. He then murdered his way through wives, mistresses, and accomplices over the next few years as he turned a lot across the street from the store into a large hotel that was designed to be used as lodging during the World's Fair. Newspapers would later dub the building the "Murder Castle," as it was discovered that many of the hotel's guests vanished without a trace. Investigations would later find human remains in the building, along with

Holmes' "Murder Castle," located in Englewood on Chicago's South Side, was not merely a torture chamber and death trap, but operated as a hotel and was home to a number of legitimate businesses on the ground floor, including a jewelry shop, drug store, cigar shop, barber, and more.

secret passageways, trap doors, and even a dissecting laboratory in the basement. The law eventually caught up with Holmes after he murdered an accomplice named Benjamin Pitezel during an insurance swindle. He also killed three of Pitezel's children while on the run from the authorities. He was captured, tried, and eventually hanged in Philadelphia.

Holmes was arrested on November 17, 1894, but his links to Chicago -- and the "Murder Castle" -- would not be explored until the following summer. Holmes' various confessions led authorities to investigate his Chicago properties, which Holmes had abandoned the previous year. Rumors had been circulating that the bodies of people who had gone missing after being connected to Holmes were buried in the cellar of the Englewood building. The police had planned to investigate the "castle" for some time but had been

Inside the Murder Castle: Holmes' gas chamber, underground crematory, and the mysterious tank in the basement that was filled with fumes that exploded and injured several firefighters and investigators

put off by the shopkeepers who were still operating on the first floor. They were reluctant to have the police digging up the basement, likely because it would be bad for business. When the bodies of two of the Pitezel children were found in Toronto, however, Inspector Fitzpatrick of Chicago's Central Detective division became determined to go ahead with the search.

Detectives and police officers entered the structure, and the news of what they found inside shocked the people of Chicago. It would be during this time that the public perception of H.H. Holmes underwent a dramatic shift. Suddenly, he was seen as something infinitely more diabolical than just a cold-blooded schemer who killed an accomplice for the money. After news emerged about what was found inside of the "Murder Castle," Holmes became a monster of mythic proportions, a creature on the order of the Devil himself.

Investigators first entered the castle on Friday night, July 19, 1895. They descended to the cellar first, and its size, measuring more than 50 by 165 feet, made a complete excavation a daunting task. After poking around by lantern light for a few hours, the men left for the night.

They returned early on Saturday morning, accompanied by a crew of city construction workers. Using picks and shovels, the men set about their work, searching for any likely spot where Holmes might have disposed of his victims.

While all of this was going on, Detective Sergeants Fitzpatrick and John Norton, accompanied by several newspaper reporters and a Pinkerton agent, ascended to the second story of the building, where Holmes kept his private chambers. They were dumbfounded by what they encountered -- a labyrinth of narrow, winding passages with doors that opened to brick walls, hidden stairways, cleverly concealed doors, blind hallways, secret panels, hidden passages, and dangerous trap doors.

The second floor also held 35 guest rooms for the hotel that Holmes operated during the Columbian Exposition. Half of them were fitted as ordinary sleeping chambers, and there were indications that they had been occupied by the various women who had worked for Holmes, by tenants during the fair, and perhaps by the unlucky females Holmes had seduced while waiting for an opportunity to kill them. Several of the rooms were without windows and could be made airtight by closing the doors. It was later discovered that some of them were lined with sheet iron and asbestos, fitted with trap doors that led to smaller rooms beneath, or were equipped with lethal gas jets that could be used to suffocate the unsuspecting occupants.

Stunned and bewildered, the investigators struggled to make sense of what they had found. It would be several more weeks before the second floor of the castle was fully surveyed and charted, and, even then, many of its bizarre features would continue to defy explanation.

However, one thing was clear -- in the middle of one of the most thriving cities in America, H.H. Holmes had managed to construct a dwelling place that rivaled a castle of horrors that could be found in any piece of lurid fiction.

On the top floor of the building, they found other grim surprises, including a clandestine vault that was only big enough for one person to stand in. The room was alleged to be a homemade "gas chamber," equipped with a chute that would carry a body directly into the basement. The investigators suddenly realized the implications of the iron-plated chamber when they found the single, scuffed mark on the inside of the door. It was a small, bare footprint that had been made by a woman who had attempted to escape the grim fate of the tiny room.

This floor also contained Holmes' private apartment, consisting of a bedroom, a bath, and two small chambers that were used as offices. The apartment was located at the front of the building, looking out over 63rd Street. In the floor of the bathroom, concealed under a heavy rug, the police found a trap door and a stairway that descended to a room about eight feet square. Two doors led off this chamber. One led to a stairway that exited out onto the street, and the other offered access to the chute that led down to the basement.

Inside Holmes' office was an immense iron stove, standing eight feet tall and measuring more than three feet in circumference. Opening its door,

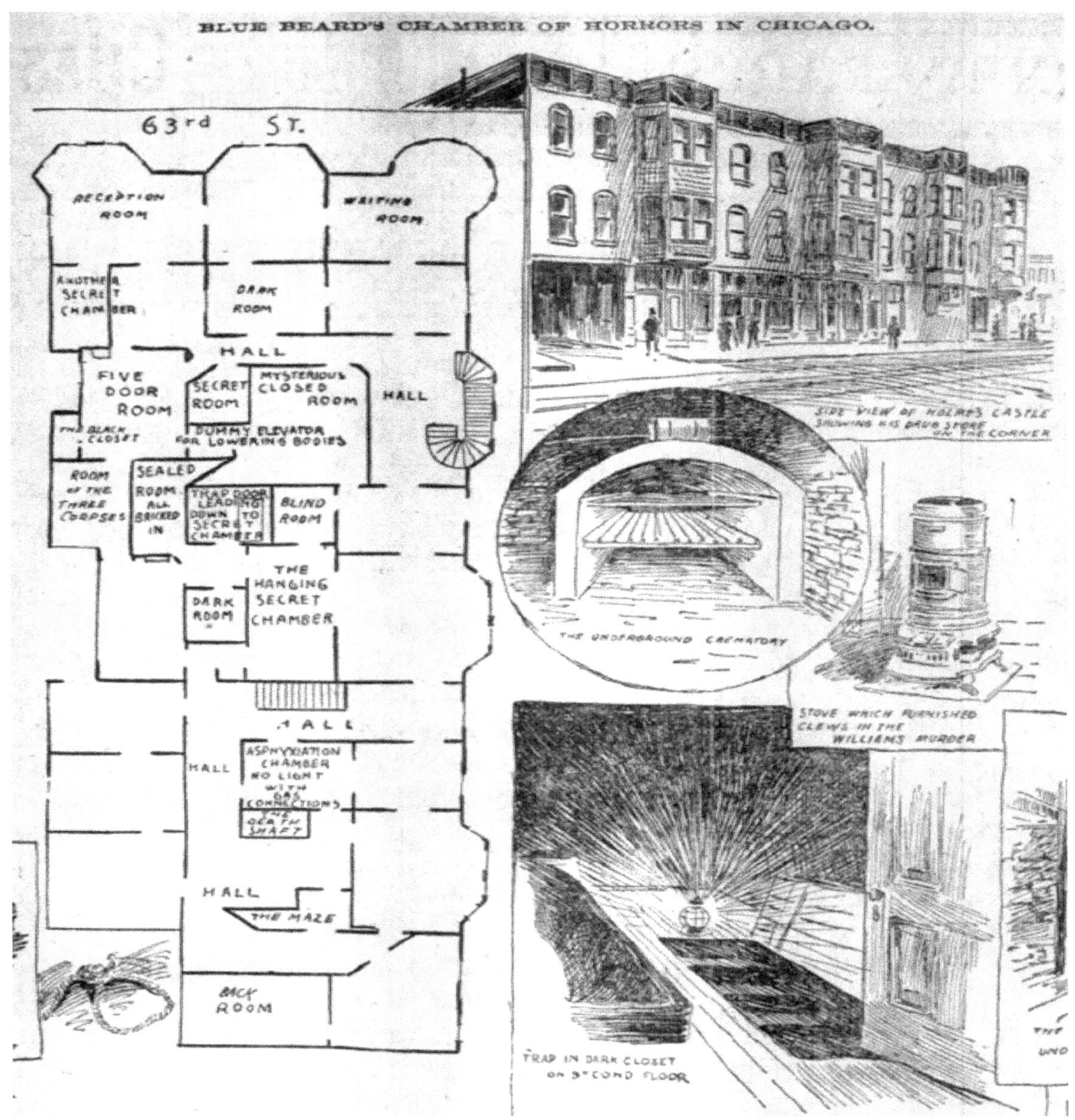

Newspaper diagram that appeared at the time of the Murder Castle's first exploration by police. The lurid and sensational articles sent hundreds of the morbid curious to Englewood to see the place for themselves — and convinced a former police office to open the place as a "murder museum."

which, as one reporter noted, was "sufficiently large to admit a human body," Sergeant Fitzpatrick began poking through the debris with his cane. Suddenly, he gasped, reached inside, and pulled out a charred object that bore a striking resemblance to a human rib bone. Pulling off his coat and rolling up his shirtsleeves, he scooped out the ashes from the stove onto the floor. Among them, they found more bone fragments, buttons from a woman's dress, and the remains of a lady's watch chain that was later determined to belong to one of Holmes' victims, a young woman named Minnie Williams.

As Fitzpatrick carefully wrapped the evidence in a handkerchief, one of the newspaper reporters took down the stovepipe and peered into the chimney. He let out a cry of disgust and then reached into the opening and pulled out a large clump of charred human hair.

By that time, the men working in the basement had made some gruesome discoveries of their own, including what was theorized to be a dissecting table that was covered with blood, surgical instruments, homemade torture devices, jars of what were believed to be poison, and a slipper and pieces of a dress that were sifted from an ash heap in a dark corner of the cellar. They also found a large pit of quicklime, which would have been capable dissolving an entire body in a matter of hours. The men searched through the pit and uncovered a portion of a skeleton. Examining the bones by lantern light, Dr. C. P. Stringfield pronounced they were almost certainly the rib cage and pelvis of a human being, which, based on their size, could only have come from a child between the ages of four and eight. Investigator believed them to be the remains of Pearl Connor, the daughter of another of Holmes' many victims.

As the search continued, detectives were convinced that a mass grave would be found in the basement. They made their way along the south wall, tapping on it at regular intervals with their tools until they discovered a hollow spot about 25 feet from the Wallace Street side. Using their picks, construction workers quickly broke through the wall. Peering into the darkness, they were able to see a mysterious wooden tank, fitted with metal pipes. One of the men squeezed into the opening and tapped on the tank with his pick. The point of it pierced the side of the tank, releasing an odor so foul that the men threw down their tools and fled from the basement.

A plumber was summoned, but, before he could arrive, three of the men went down into the cellar to see if the fumes had dispersed. As they made their way across the dark chamber, one of the men struck a match against the wall.

And the strange wooden tank exploded.

The blast shook the building, sending the terrified first-floor shopkeepers running out into the street. An alarm was raised, and, within minutes, Fire Chief Joseph Kenyon was on the scene with Engine No. 51 and Truck No. 20. By then, several of the workmen had gone down into the basement to search for their comrades. The men were buried in piles of debris, but no one was seriously injured.

Before the firefighters could set up their equipment, the fire had burned itself out. Chief Kenyon decided to open the tank and let the noxious fumes dissipate. He and several of his men made their way into the basement but were so overcome by the vapors that they barely managed to stagger back up to the street. Kenyon was most affected by the gas, and, according to the *New York World* newspaper, "He was dragged out and carried upstairs, and for two hours acted like one demented." He remained delirious for nearly two hours and, at one point, even seemed close to death. He finally recovered later in the afternoon. What the gas might have been, or what the mysterious tank might have been used for, remains a mystery.

By Sunday morning, the air in the basement was breathable again, and investigators and crewmembers went back to work. However, their efforts were hampered by the throng of curiosity-seekers who had swarmed the building, drawn by the lurid newspaper

THE HOLMES CASTLE

The Weird Story of an Artful Murderer who Actually Built the Tomb for a Dozen of his Victims

One of the wildly inaccurate stories that began to appear about Holmes and his Murder Castle

headlines about Holmes' "Murder Castle." The police eventually managed to clear everyone out, but not before many of them had helped themselves to souvenirs, including personal letters and files from Holmes' private office. It will never be known if one of these intruders made off with a vital clue that might have identified one of the people who vanished during the

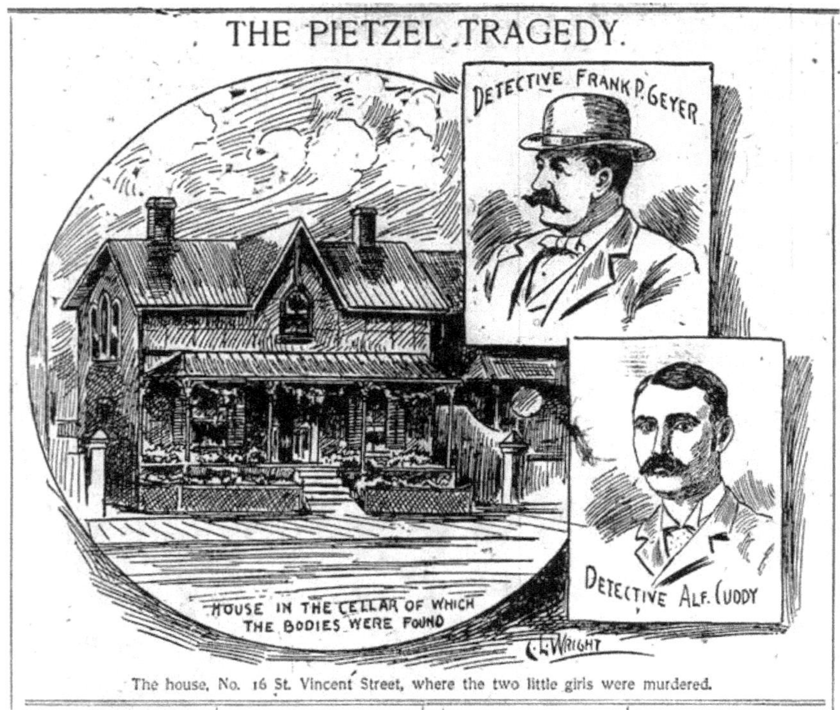

The house, No. 16 St. Vincent Street, where the two little girls were murdered.

While the list of Holmes' possible victims was long, there were many to which he confessed or could be linked — like those of the Pitezel sisters, who were found buried in a cellar in Canada.

Columbian Exposition, feared to be a victim of Holmes -- but never proven.

The only new discovery made in the basement on Sunday was that of a bloodstained dress that Sergeant Fitzpatrick found in an ash heap in the northeast corner. The crew doubled their efforts on Monday and turned up a woman's shoe, the broken lid of an opera-glass case, and some skeletal fragments. Then, at the west end of the cellar, they came upon a padlocked storage room, which they promptly broke open. The floor of the small room was littered with rubbish, and underneath, the police found a length of stout rope that had been tied at one end into a loop. The opposite end, which was darkly stained with what appeared to be blood, had been tied into a hangman's noose. A reporter for the *Philadelphia Inquirer* wrote, "The length of rope is such that were the plaited loop attached to the upstairs wall of the secret dumb-waiter shaft, a body hanging from the noose would just clear the bottom of the shaft. This coincidence convinced some of the detectives that Holmes' alleged victims had been pushed through the upstairs door in the dumb-waiter and strangled to death in the shaft below."

As news of the castle's grisly discoveries continued to spread, the authorities slowly realized that they were dealing with a frightening new phenomenon -- a killer who was so unique in their experience that they were unable to give him a name. A Chicago journalist came up with the term "multi-murderer," but it would be nearly 100 years before criminologists coined the term "serial killer" to describe a monster like H.H. Holmes.

With each day that passed, more horror was realized by the people of Chicago. And with each passing day, the list of Holmes' possible victims grew.

The list included Emmeline Cigrand, a lovely young stenographer who had gone to work for Holmes in 1892 and disappeared a short time later, and Emily Van Tassel, a pretty grocery store cashier who had vanished soon after striking up an acquaintance with Holmes in 1893. There was also Wilfred Cole, a wealthy lumberman from Baltimore who had traveled to Chicago on unspecified business with Holmes and was never seen again. A physician named Russler, who was allegedly a close friend of Holmes, had vanished in 1892. Harry Walker, a young man who had gone to work as a private secretary for Holmes, had disappeared in 1893, a few months after a $15,000 life insurance had been taken out on him with Holmes as the beneficiary. The police also wondered about the whereabouts of a wealthy and attractive widow named Mrs. Lee, who had kept company with Holmes and then vanished. The list also included three missing members of the Gorky family: a middle-aged widow named Kate, who ran a restaurant on the first floor of Holmes' building during the time of the Columbian Exposition; her lovely sister, Liz, and her pretty teen-aged daughter, Anna. There was also

an indeterminate number of female clerical workers who had allegedly vanished after taking jobs at the castle, including a beautiful Boston girl named Mabel Barrett, a 16-year-old stenographer named Kelly, and perhaps dozens of others. One report stated that Holmes had "employed more than 100 young women during his years in Englewood." How many of these young women were never heard from again remains a mystery to this day.

Among the many crimes attributed to Holmes during the first frenzied days of the exposure for the "Murder Castle" was the murder of Mrs. Patrick Quinlan, the wife of the building's janitor. The front-page story of the July 25 edition of the *Chicago Inter-Ocean* asked, "Are more murders to be added to the list of Holmes' atrocities? Is the wife of Pat Quinlan alive? Did Holmes the arch-fiend make away with her, and are her bones rotting in some cellar buried in quick lime?"

Less than 24 hours after the newspaper posed these chilling questions, Mrs. Quinlan showed up at Chicago police headquarters and was taken into custody, along with her husband. They were arrested on charges of conspiring with Holmes, and both were subjected to relentless questioning. After countless hours of interrogation, Mrs. Quinlan finally broke down and confessed to her

Pat Quinlan

knowledge of at least some of Holmes' insurance scams.

Her husband, however, refused to admit to anything. Patrick Quinlan sobbed to reporters after one brutal interrogation, "I am innocent. I knew Holmes and worked for him. All these people you say were murdered, I knew, and when they went away, as Holmes claimed, I thought it was funny. You say I helped him to commit murder, but I did not. I am innocent, and I cannot tell you what you claim I know. Let me alone. I am innocent!"

Police Chief Badenoch, however, scoffed at Quinlan's protestations. He stated flatly that the man was a murderer. At the time of his arrest, the janitor had been carrying a big iron ring that contained 37 keys to various locks throughout the castle, even to doors that hid Holmes' secret rooms and "asphyxiation chambers." No one with that sort of access to the innermost passages of the building could have been ignorant of deadly secrets like acid vats, quicklime pits, dissecting tables, a private crematorium, and scattered piles of human bones.

Quinlan was either a willing accomplice or was one of the stupidest human beings on earth.

The same evening that Quinlan was arrested, on July 26, the police searched his apartment and found a letter that had been sent to him by Holmes, who was in prison in Philadelphia at the time. The letter was written on two scraps of common Manila paper and looked remarkably as if it were meant to be found and read by the police. Holmes apparently tried to establish alibis for himself and Quinlan with the letter. It was written on June 18 - before an investigator named Frank Geyer discovered the body of one of Benjamin Pitezel's children at a small cottage near Indianapolis. It read:

Dear Pat:

Among their other fool theories, they think you took the Pitezel boy to Michigan and either left him there or put him out of the way. I have always told them that I never asked you to do anything illegal, but they are bull-headed. October 19, I saw you at the factory, I think. Can you show where you were all the rest of the month? If they question you, or threaten to arrest you, tell them everything there is to tell about this or any other matter. They may want to know if you were in Cincinnati or Indianapolis about October 12. It is well for you to know where you were working. I am awfully sorry, Pat, for I have always tried to make things easy for you. When Minnie killed her sister, I needed you in the worst way, but would not drag you into it.

Note: Minnie Williams and her sister, Nannie, were two victims of Holmes but he later claimed that Minnie killed her sister because she was jealous of a sexual relationship that she had with Holmes. He claimed that in a fit of anger, Minnie hit her sister with a chair and killed her. Holmes then placed the body in a trunk and dumped it in Lake Michigan. He went on to say that Minnie fled to Europe soon after. More likely, both women were destroyed in the basement acid vat.

The letter continued:

If the detectives go to New York, as I want them to, they would find where Minnie took them by boat. I have done no killing, Pat. One by one, they are finding them alive. Minnie will not come here as long as there is any danger of her being arrested. A Boston man knows where she is, and her guardian (Messie H. Watt) will, at the safe and proper time, go to her. Let your wife write me anything you wish, not oftener than twice a month, directing H.H. Holmes, County Prison, Tenth and Reed Streets, Philadelphia. I cannot write many letters to you. I am doing all I can for all. Expect to hear shortly from you. Give my love to your wife and Cora. Tell her I have her picture in my room and thank her for

Holmes in his prison cell in Philadelphia, from which he wrote the letters to Pat Quinlan.

it. I have a tame mouse and spider to keep me company. My feed is the worst part here. Clarence Phillips' restaurant at its worst would be fine compared with it. I only eat once a day. Shall be out of it sooner than you expect. They kept Mrs. P. shut up here for six months when we would have let her out on bail. Made a fool of her. Write soon and free. Ask any questions you want to. Georgiana is visiting her mother. Went about two weeks ago.

With regards to all,

H.H. Holmes

The discovery of the letter, despite its claim that Quinlan was not involved in anything illegal, made the police even more convinced that the janitor was involved in Holmes' operations. Chief Badenoch told reporters on July 27, "I think I will be able to wrest a confession from Quinlan before long. I do not intend to let him turn state's evidence, if I can help it, although I believe he is weakening to such an extent that should such a suggestion be made to him, he would grasp it eagerly and at once."

On July 28, astounding new evidence came from another witness that seemed to firmly cement Quinlan's role as an accomplice in Holmes' crimes. This testimony convinced the police of the man's guilt, but in the end, it was also what ultimately freed him from custody.

According to newspaper reports that appeared that afternoon, Sergeant Fitzpatrick was allegedly able to track down four skeletons that had been removed from the castle under the direction of Holmes and Quinlan. The skeletons were said to have been prepared by a man named Charles M. Chappell, who had first met Holmes in the summer of 1892. Chappell had seen a newspaper advertisement that Holmes had posted, looking for a machinist, and had applied for the job. Chappell was soon hired and had worked for several months when

Holmes asked him if he could mount a skeleton. Chappell told him that he could, and so Holmes led him to a dark room in the center of the second floor of the castle. They walked into the chamber, and, using a lantern, Holmes pointed out the body of a man on the floor. Chappell stated, "There was considerable flesh on the lower limbs, but the arms were practically denuded of flesh." Chappell took the arm bones and skull away with him that night, and Holmes delivered the rest of the skeleton to the machinist's house the following day, which was October 1, 1892.

On January 2, 1893, Chappell claimed that Holmes asked him to articulate another skeleton for him. Another trip to the dark room revealed another skeleton, this time that of a female. This body had much more flesh on it than the other, and when he described its condition to the police, Chappell said, "The body looked like that of a jackrabbit when had been skinned by splitting the skin down the face and rolling it back off the entire body. In some places, considerable amounts of the flesh had been taken off with it."

Even though the newspapers reported that Chappell had turned over an entire skeleton to the police, he actually provided only a skull. The reports also erroneously claimed that detectives recovered the skeletons of two adult women -- one from the home of a West Side physician and the other

Newspaper illustration of Charles M. Chappell, the mechanic who articulated the skeletons of Holmes' victims

from the LaSalle Medical School -- plus a trunk containing an assortment of "human relics," including an arm bone, a hand, and a skull. Not surprisingly, the sensational press published these wild rumors as fact. In truth, the bodies and "human relics" never turned up.

Charles Chappell did exist, however, and he did tell the police about the skeletons that he allegedly articulated for Holmes. Holmes then sold the skeletons to doctors, medical schools, and private buyers. Perhaps most damning in his allegations was the testimony that he gave against Patrick Quinlan, whom Chappell claimed knew all about Holmes' illegal activities. Chappell stated that while he was working on the remains for Holmes, Quinlan was on the premises and appeared, in the machinist's mind, to be Holmes' "trusted man."

Chappell also led the police to another witness who could vouch for Quinlan's intimacy with Holmes' crimes -- a black man named Cephas Humphrey, who drove an express wagon. Humphrey told detectives that one day in June 1893, Holmes summoned him to the "castle" and asked him to take a trunk and a box to Union Station. Holmes told him, "I want you after the stuff about dark as I do not care to have the neighbors see it go away."

Humphrey returned later that evening and he claimed that he was taken to the dark room in the center of the second floor by none other than Patrick Quinlan. Humphrey described the room as "an awful-looking place. There were no windows in it at all and only a heavy door opening into it. It made my flesh creep to go in there. I felt as if something was wrong."

Humphrey described a large box there that looked like a casing ordinarily used for a coffin. He carried it downstairs and started to stand it on end on the sidewalk, but as he did so, he heard a sharp tapping noise coming from above and behind him. He looked up and saw Holmes peering out of a second-floor window. He told Humphrey not to stand the box on end but rather to lay it down flat. After loading the box into his wagon, Humphrey retrieved the trunk and then was instructed to take them both to Union Station and leave them on a certain platform. He was told not to say anything to anyone but simply leave the packages. A man there was expecting them and knew what to do with them. The express driver vaguely remembered that the box was supposed to go to Philadelphia, but he could not remember where the trunk was sent.

According to the newspapers, the police were excited to hear of these new developments and felt they now had Quinlan securely in their grasp. More and more evidence seemed to be piling up against him, including the fact that he was a bricklayer by trade, which seemed to suggest that he may have assisted in building the secret vaults for Holmes in the cellar of the "Murder Castle."

Chief Badenoch publicly stated that he believed Holmes had corrupted Quinlan, who was known as an honest man before he met Holmes. He had worked for Holmes for $2 per day but rarely did any real labor, acting more as a confidential agent. This was the reason detectives believed that he was aware of what Holmes was doing. Badenoch felt that with the new information that they had received, Quinlan would soon confess to his role in the many murders of H.H. Holmes.

Chief Badenoch had no idea at the time that he made these statements that he would be forced to release Pat Quinlan from custody a few days later.

At this same time, the police were finally wrapping up their search of the "Murder Castle." Convinced that the building had yielded its darkest secrets, they halted their search on Monday, August 5. The only question that now remained was what to do with the place. Some called for its immediate demolition. The building was a "death trap" -- and not just for the unlucky victims who never left the place. E.F. Laughlin, an inspector for the Chicago Department of Buildings, made a tour of the "castle" and was appalled by its shoddy construction. He wrote in a report, "The structural parts of the inside are all weak and dangerous. Built of the poorest and cheapest kind of material... All dividing partitions between flats are combustible... The sanitary condition of the building is horrible." His final recommendation was that the building should be condemned.

To others, the destruction of the castle seemed a terrible waste. The place might not be fit for habitation, but there were other uses to which it might be put. On July 28, nearly 5,000 people had flocked to Englewood, hoping for a glimpse of the castle's ghastly interior and its "torture chamber," "suffocation vault," and "burial cellar." The following week, the *New York Times* published a story headlined "Knows How it Feels to Smother," about a Chicago man named William Barnes, who locked himself inside a jeweler's vault because he wanted to "learn the sensations of some of Holmes' victims."

It was clear that the "Devil" had a firm grip on Chicago's imagination and that there was good money to be made from such a morbid fascination, as an enterprising former policeman named A.M. Clark was quick to realize. Even before the police had called a halt to the investigation, Clark had arranged to lease the building from its court-appointed receiver. On Sunday, August 11, he made his announcement to the press. Beginning that week, the castle would be opened as a tourist attraction

HOLMES CONFESSES 27 MURDERS

THE MOST AWFUL STORY OF MODERN TIMES TOLD BY THE FIEND IN HUMAN SHAPE.

Every Detail of His Fearful Crimes Told by the Man Who Admits He Is Turning Into the Shape of the Devil.

THE TALE OF THE GREATEST CRIMINAL IN HISTORY

: The following statement was written by me in Philadelphia County Prison for the Philadelphia Inquirer as a true & accurate confession in all particulars. It is the only confession

- a "murder museum" with an admission charge of 15 cents per person and guided tours conducted by Detective John Norton, who had first-hand knowledge of the case.

As Clark was preparing his new "murder museum" for its grand opening, the police received unfortunate news in the Pat Quinlan investigation. Quinlan and his wife were still in custody, and no matter how the police questioned them, both refused to admit to any part in the murders that Holmes committed. Mrs. Quinlan had confessed to knowing about Holmes' insurance schemes, but her husband was adamant about the fact that he had done nothing illegal.

Detectives were sure that the witness statements from the machinist, Charles Chappell, and the express driver, Cephas Humphrey, would be enough to push Quinlan into a full confession -- but they couldn't have been more wrong.

It would be the family of Charles Chappell, who would first call his testimony into question. Aside from the fact that the police had never recovered the skeletons that Chappell claimed he had articulated for Holmes, his own family dismissed his statement as the ramblings of a delusional drunk. They claimed that his story was something that he made up in hopes of cadging free drinks for a recitation of the tale he told the police. Chappell had done some work for Holmes, but whether he actually constructed any skeletons for him seemed more and more unlikely every day. This also caused authorities to question his identification of Pat Quinlan as Holmes' "trusted man," as well. With nothing more than suspicion, the police were forced to let Quinlan go. He never confessed to any wrongdoing, and no hard evidence ever emerged against him. Two years later, Quinlan attempted to sue the police department for false arrest, but the case was thrown out of court.

Could this have been because the courts felt just as the police authorities did -- that Patrick Quinlan knew much more than he was saying, even though no one could prove it? It seems possible and, in fact, questions have continued to be raised about the role that Quinlan had in Holmes' crimes, especially considering what happened next.

Less than two weeks after it was vacated by the police, H.H. Holmes' "Murder Castle," which had been newly remodeled as a tourist attraction under the management of A.M. Clark, was ready to admit its first paying customers. However, around midnight on Monday, August 19 -- just days after Pat Quinlan was released from custody -- Clark's get-rich-quick scheme literally went up in smoke.

No one ever found out how the fire got started, and its cause remains a mystery to this day. Some saw it as an act of divine retribution as God purged Chicago of Holmes' "chamber of horrors." Others suggested that perhaps it had been a resident of Englewood, ashamed of the blemish that the castle had created on the city's reputation. The police, on the other hand, took another view. They suspected that a confederate of Holmes' had torched the place to conceal incriminating evidence that the investigators had overlooked.

Whatever the source of the fire, it made short work of the "murder museum." At precisely 12:13 a.m., a night watchman at the Western Indiana railroad crossing named George J. Myler spotted flames coming through the building's roof. Before he could turn in the alarm, a series of explosions rocked the building, blowing out the windows of the candy shop on the first floor. By the time the first fire engines arrived, the blaze was nearly out of control. A half-hour later, part of the roof collapsed, taking down part of the castle's rear wall. Under the direction of Chief Kenyon, the firefighters managed to keep the fire from spreading to the frame houses at the rear. Regardless, by the time the blaze was extinguished -- about an hour and a half after it was first reported -- much of the structure had been consumed.

Although the first-floor shops sustained only minimal damage, the two upper stories of the building were completely gutted. The new "murder museum" was a blackened shell, and

A.M. Clark was out of business for good. The fire did not destroy the castle completely, though. Even though the second and third floors were sealed off, and their windows boarded over, the first floor remained in operation for many years. A sign shop and a bookstore operated at 601-603 West 63rd Street until the building was sold in 1937. A year later, the building razed to make way for the U.S. Post Office that still stands at the site today. The owners, an elderly woman named Emma Morrison and several other people who were not named, were paid the sum of $61,000 for the land.

An immediate suspect in the arson fire was Patrick Quinlan, who had just been released from custody, but the police could not make the charges stick. They did manage to track Quinlan to another building that was owned by Holmes, this one located on the northwest side of Chicago.

On August 21, several newspapers reported that another Holmes site had been discovered about 10 miles from the "Murder Castle." It was described as a small, glass-bending factory that was one-story high, 20 feet wide and 150 feet long, located near a two-and-a-half-story house. The location of the structure was given as "where 65 Sobieski Street ought to be, near the tracks of the Northwestern Railroad, a little northwest of the North Robey Street crossing." Robey Street is called Damen Avenue today, and Sobieski is a very small road - only about a quarter-mile long - between Robey and Hoyne, near Fullerton Avenue.

Neighbors identified Holmes as the owner of the building, which was closed and boarded up by 1895. They had not seen Holmes in some time, but they did recognize a photograph of Pat Quinlan, who they said had come to the building a few days before and had removed a number of boxes and bundles from the place. Inside, the police found nothing but scrap metal, a wall of furnaces, and a handful of papers, all bearing Quinlan's signature. The police suspected that Holmes had used the building for some of his cremations, but they couldn't prove anything. They had discovered the building by tracing a Brink's express company order that had directed them to pick up a box at No. 65 Sobieski Street on December 6, 1894. Directions were given to stop at the glass company building to await further instructions. The order was signed by P.B. Quinlan. The express driver who called that day remembered being taken to the frame house at the rear of the factory. From there, a large box and several bundles were taken to the general depot of the express company, where they were shipped out two days later. What may have been in the boxes, or where they were finally taken, remains a mystery.

Once again, more suspicion was directed towards Pat Quinlan, but again, no evidence of anything illegal could be obtained. Had Quinlan been

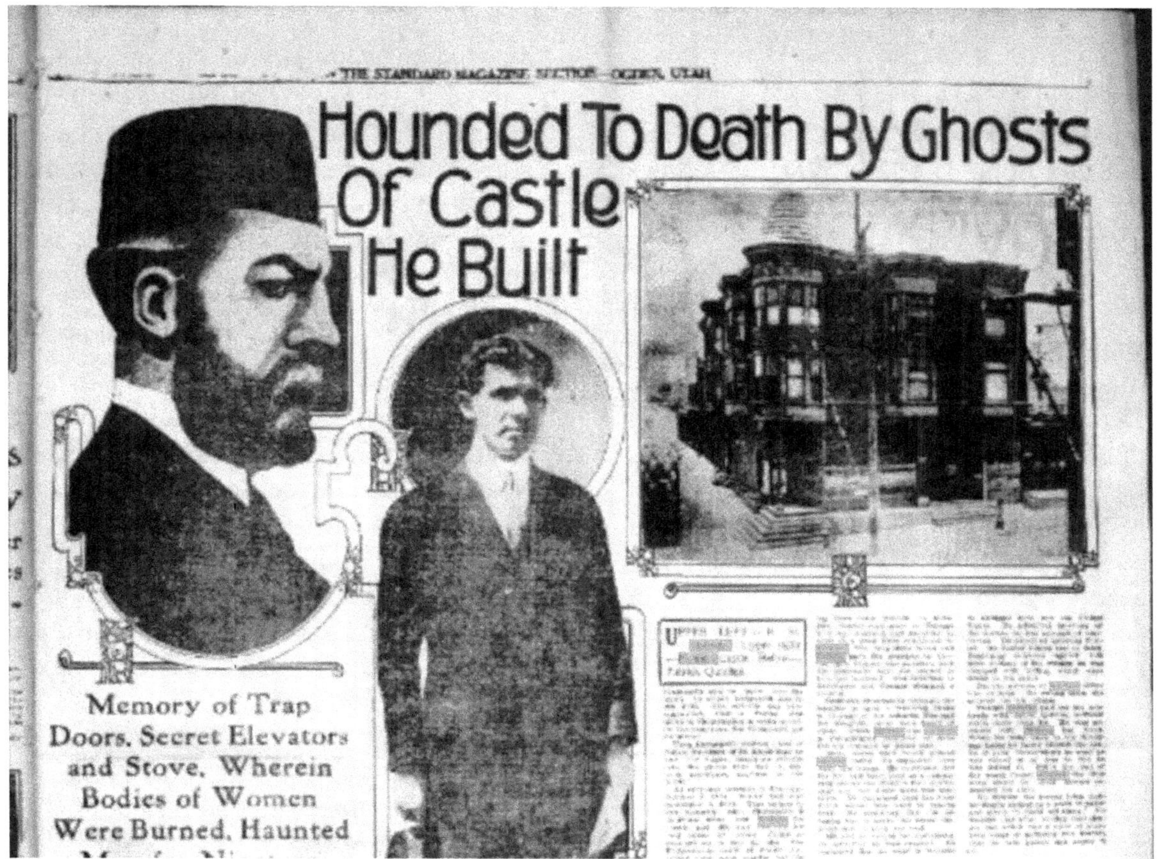

involved in the fire that destroyed most of the "Murder Castle?" Had he disposed of evidence from the Sobieski Street location? Or was he simply an unknowing, clueless, and accidental "accomplice?"

There were those, in addition to the police, who believed that Patrick Quinlan was anything but innocent. One of those people was Jonathan Belknap, the granduncle of Myrta Belknap, a wife of Holmes who lived in Wilmette. He later stated that he believed that Quinlan had once tried to kill him, acting under orders from Holmes. He recalled, "I knew Holmes was a scoundrel, and I had been warned not to be alone with him. I did not want to stay in his house overnight, but he urged it, and I could not well get out of it. During the day, Holmes showed me the house and tried to get me to go up on the roof with him, but I would not. He went away that night, and I went to bed and carefully locked the door. I did not sleep well, and late in the night, I was awakened by cautious footsteps in the hall and heard someone try to open the door. I lay quiet, and presently, there came a rap.

I asked what was up, and Pat Quinlan answered that he wanted to come in and sleep with me. I have no doubt that if I had gone on the roof with Holmes, or had let Quinlan into my room, I would not be here now."

Jonathan Belknap believed that Quinlan was a killer, and so did many members of the Chicago Police Department, but Quinlan always publicly maintained his innocence. Yes, he had been the janitor and caretaker of the "Murder Castle," and yes, he had even helped construct some of the secret trap doors and lined rooms with asbestos, but he had no idea what they were to be used for. He was innocent of murder, and he stated that many times -- but was he really?

When Quinlan committed suicide in 1914, he left a note that contained one simple phrase: "I could not sleep." It was the final statement, most believed, of a man who had been tortured by his own conscience for many years.

After his unsuccessful lawsuit against the police department, Quinlan left Chicago and returned to his home in Portland, Michigan. There, he settled into a quiet life but one that was continually plagued by other people's curiosity. He often told his wife and his friends that he was constantly being stared at on the streets. People watched him and wondered about what dark deeds he had committed. Quinlan said that while the rest of the world forgot about H.H. Holmes, the curiosity-seekers of Portland, Michigan, never forgot about Pat Quinlan.

For 19 years, Quinlan was unable to sleep. At night, he would awake with a start and find himself covered in sweat, his friends later said. He would call for help, and when a light would be turned on, he would recount how he was attacked in his sleep by strange hallucinations -- ghosts of the many victims of H.H. Holmes.

Finally, when he could stand it no more, Quinlan swallowed a bottle of poison and died on the floor of his Michigan home, his hastily scrawled note by his side. Was he an innocent man, driven to suicide because of guilt over what he should have known -- or was he a guilty man, hounded to his death by the spirits of those whom he helped to send to an early grave?

The truth will likely never be known.

MORBID CURIOUS
Contributors NO.1

Amanda R. Woomer

Writer, anthropologist, and former international English teacher, Amanda R. Woomer was born and raised in Buffalo, NY. She is a contributor to the award-winning Haunted Magazine and the owner of Spook-Eats, a travel website where she visits haunted restaurants, bars, and hotels in search of spirits of all kinds. She is the author of The Haunted Atlas of Western New York, THE SPIRIT GUIDE: America's Haunted Breweries, Distilleries, and Wineries, and The Cryptid ABC Book, book one in the Creepy Books for Creepy Kids series. Follow her spooky adventures at spookeats.com.

Rene' Kruse

Rene' Kruse grew up in small towns on the Great Plains and Texas but has lived in Southwestern Pennsylvania for the past 25 years. She holds a PhD from Texas A&M and teaches Applied Engineering and Technology at California University of Pennsylvania. Rene' has been fascinated in ghosts and all things haunted for as long as she can remember and has been actively investigating haunted sites for over 35 years. She is the co-author of several books, including AND HELL FOLLOWED WITH IT, A PALE HORSE WAS DEATH, and FEAR THE REAPER. She is a longtime speaker and contributor to the Haunted America Conference.

Trevelyn Florence-Thomas

Trevelyn Florence-Thomas is a native Midwesterner, born and raised in the small, rural community of Jacksonville, Illinois. She developed a love for reading and writing at a very young age. As a kindergarten student, she received recognition and won her first literary award for her short poem titled "Pink Snow." More recently, she served as a columnist for local publications such as the Jacksonville Journal Courier and The Source newspaper. Throughout her life, Trevelyn has cultivated an interest in the paranormal and things that go bump in the night. She holds a Bachelor of Arts degree from the University of Illinois at Urbana-Champaign and a Master of Arts degree in Sociology from Fisk University in Nashville, Tennessee. Trevelyn is a firm believer in both spirituality and the supernatural.

Michelle L. Hamilton

Michelle L. Hamilton earned her MA in History from San Diego State University. Hamilton is the author or editor of several books including *"I Would Still Be Drowned in Tears": Spiritualism in Abraham Lincoln's White House* and *Mary Ball Washington: The Mother of George Washington*. Her latest book is *Civil War Ghosts* published by Haunted Road Media. A lifelong student of history, Hamilton has worked as a docent at several museums across the county. She is currently the manager of the Mary Washington House in Fredericksburg, VA. You can follow her at her blog Paranormal History at https://paranormalhist.blogspot.com/

Troy Taylor

Troy Taylor is an author of books on ghosts, hauntings, true crime, the unexplained, and the supernatural in America. He is also the founder of American Hauntings Ink, which offers books, ghost tours, events, and weekend excursions. He was born and raised in the Midwest and currently divides his time between Illinois and the far-flung reaches of America.

Special Thanks

April Slaughter
Lisa Taylor Horton and Lux
Kaylan Schardan
Cody Beck
Lois Taylor
Orrin Taylor
Rene Kruse
Rachael Horath
Elyse and Thomas Reihner
Bethany Horath
Becky Ray
John Winterbauer
Maggie and Packy Lundholm
Tom and Michelle Bonadurer
Susan Kelly and Amy Bouyear
David Rotenstein
And the entire crew of American Hauntings